Guide to Publishing in Psychology Journals

Guide to Publishing in Psychology Journals

Edited by

Robert J. Sternberg

Department of Psychology, Yale University

CAMBRIDGE
UNIVERSITY PRESS

PUBLISHED BY THE PRESS SYNDICATE OF THE UNIVERSITY OF CAMBRIDGE
The Pitt Building, Trumpington Street, Cambridge, United Kingdom

CAMBRIDGE UNIVERSITY PRESS
The Edinburgh Building, Cambridge CB2 2RU, UK   http://www.cup.cam.ac.uk
40 West 20th Street, New York, NY 10011-4211, USA   http://www.cup.org
10 Stamford Road, Oakleigh, Melbourne 3166, Australia
Ruiz de Alarcón 13, 28014 Madrid, Spain

First published 2000

Printed in the United States of America

Typeface New Aster 9.75/13.5 pt.   *System* QuarkXPress™   [HT]

A catalog record for this book is available from the British Library

Library of Congress Cataloging-in-Publication Data is available

ISBN   0 521 59447 2   hardback
ISBN   0 521 59460 X   paperback

Contents

Preface

For psychologists who pursue a career in scholarship, there is one more certainty beyond death and taxes: rejected articles. Strongly refereed journals have high rejection rates and so it is almost inevitable that, sooner or later, usually sooner, one will get an editor's letter rejecting a submitted article. Even most articles that ultimately are accepted first were rejected. In some cases, the editor gave the author a chance to resubmit. In other cases, the author simply submitted the article to another journal. In either case, the article was rejected before it was accepted.

Outright acceptances are quite rare. When I was editor of the *Psychological Bulletin*, for example, our outright acceptance rate for initial submissions was probably about 2%.

The goal of this book is to offer authors guidance in how to write better articles and thereby improve their chances for acceptance. The book is divided into 14 chapters, including a final integrative chapter, with each of the first 13 chapters covering a different aspect of the article-writing process, including writing an empirical article, writing a literature review, titles and abstracts, introductions, theories and hypotheses, experimental design, data analysis, results, discussions, citations and references, writing for reviewers, reading reviews, and methods.

A unique feature of this book is that all chapter authors have been editors or associate editors of major psychological journals, so that they are in a good position to write about writing articles. In writing their chapters for this book, all of these authors have written for diverse audiences, from beginning graduate students to seasoned professionals.

This book is not intended to repeat information contained in the *Publication Manual of the American Psychological Association* (4th ed., 1994) or in guides to writing papers, such as Sternberg (1993). Rather, the book is intended to go beyond the mechanics of writing articles to the higher order issues of how to use these mechanics in an effective and productive manner.

I am grateful to Julia Hough for contracting the book, to Sai Durvasula for help with manuscript preparation, and to the American Psychological Association, which has given me the opportunity to edit two of its journals and thereby to learn first-hand about the journal-editing process.

REFERENCES

American Psychological Association (1994). *Publication manual of the American Psychological Association* (4th ed.). Washington, DC: American Psychological Association.
Sternberg, R. J. (1993). *The psychologist's companion* (3rd ed.). New York: Cambridge University Press.

PART ONE

INTRODUCTION

Chapter 1

Writing an Empirical Article

DARYL J. BEM

You have conducted a study and analyzed the data. Now it is time to write. To publish. To tell the world what you have learned. The purpose of this book is to enhance the chances that some journal editor will let you do so.

If you are new to this enterprise, you might find it helpful to consult two additional sources of information. For detailed information on the proper format of a journal article, see the *Publication Manual of the American Psychological Association* (APA, 1994) and recent articles in the particular journal to which you plan to submit your manuscript. The *Publication Manual* also devotes 15 pages each to two topics that are not discussed in this chapter: the rules of English grammar and the appropriate terms to use when referring to gender, ethnicity, or sexual orientation. For renewing your acquaintance with the stylistic elements of English prose, you can read Chapter 2 of the *Publication Manual* or any one of several style manuals. I recommend *The Elements of Style* by Strunk and White (1999). It is brief, witty, and inexpensive.

As noted in the Preface, this book focuses on the report of an empirical study, but the general writing suggestions included in this chapter apply as well to the theoretical articles, literature reviews, and methodological contributions that also appear in the professional journals.[1]

---

[1] Some of the material in this chapter has been adapted from Bem (1987, 1995).

PLANNING IT

Which Article Should You Write?

There are two possible articles you can write: (a) the article you planned to write when you designed your study or (b) the article that makes the most sense now that you have seen the results. They are rarely the same, and the correct answer is (b).

The conventional view of the research process is that we first derive a set of hypotheses from a theory, design and conduct a study to test these hypotheses, analyze the data to see if they were confirmed or disconfirmed, and then chronicle this sequence of events in the journal article. If this is how our enterprise actually proceeded, we could write most of the article before we collected the data. We could write the introduction and method sections completely, prepare the results section in skeleton form, leaving spaces to be filled in by the specific numerical results, and have two possible discussion sections ready to go, one for positive results, the other for negative results.

But this is not how our enterprise actually proceeds. Psychology is more exciting than that, and the best journal articles are informed by the actual empirical findings from the opening sentence. Accordingly, before writing your article, you need to *analyze your data*. Herewith, a brief sermonette on the topic.

Analyzing Your Data. Once upon a time, psychologists observed behavior directly, often for sustained periods of time. No longer. Now, the higher the investigator goes up the tenure ladder, the more remote he or she typically becomes from the grounding observations of our science. If you are already a successful research psychologist, then you probably haven't seen a live human participant for some time. Your graduate assistant assigns the running of a study to a bright undergraduate who writes the computer program that collects the data automatically. And like the modern dentist, the modern psychologist rarely even sees the data until they have been cleaned by human or computer hygienists.

To compensate for this remoteness from our participants, let us at least become intimately familiar with the record of their behavior: the data. Examine them from every angle. Analyze the sexes separately. Make up new composite indices. If a datum suggests a new hypothesis, try to find further evidence for it elsewhere in the data. If you see dim traces of interesting patterns, try to reorganize the data to bring them into bolder relief. If there are participants you don't like, or trials, observers, or interviewers who gave you anomalous results, place them aside temporarily and see if any coherent patterns emerge. Go on a fishing expedition for something – anything – interesting.

No, this is not immoral. In fact, there are now textbooks and computer packages explicitly designed for this kind of exploratory data analysis. The rules of scientific and statistical inference that we over-learn in graduate school apply to the "Context of Justification." They tell us what we can legitimately conclude in the articles we write for public consumption, and they give our readers criteria for deciding whether or not to believe us. But in the "Context of Discovery," there are no formal rules, only heuristics or strategies. How does one discover a new phenomenon? Smell a good idea? Have a brilliant insight into behavior? Create a new theory? In the confining context of an empirical study, there is only one strategy for discovery: exploring the data.

Yes, there is a danger. Spurious findings can emerge by chance, and we need to be cautious about anything we discover in this way. In limited cases, there are statistical techniques that correct for this danger. But there are no statistical correctives for overlooking an important discovery because we were insufficiently attentive to the data. Let us err on the side of discovery.

Reporting the Findings. When you are through exploring, you may conclude that the data are not strong enough to justify your new insights formally, but at least you are now ready to design the "right" study. If you still plan to report the current data, you may wish to mention the new insights tentatively, stating honestly that they remain to be tested adequately. Alternatively, the data may be strong enough and reliable enough to justify recentering your article around the new findings and subordinating or even ignoring your original hypotheses.

This is *not* advice to suppress negative results. If your study was genuinely designed to test hypotheses that derive from a theory or are of wide general interest for some other reason, then they should remain the focus of your article. The integrity of the scientific enterprise requires the reporting of disconfirming results – even if only to warn other researchers about pursuing the same fruitless path.

But this requirement assumes that somebody out there cares about the hypotheses. Many respectable studies are explicitly exploratory or are launched from speculations of the "I-wonder-if . . . " variety. If your study is one of these, then nobody cares if you were wrong. Contrary to the conventional wisdom, science does not care how clever or clairvoyant you were at guessing your results ahead of time. Scientific integrity does not require you to lead your readers through all your wrongheaded hunches only to show – voila! – they were wrongheaded. A journal article should not be a personal history of your stillborn thoughts.

Your overriding purpose is to tell the world what you have learned from your study. If your results suggest a compelling framework for their presentation, adopt it and make the most instructive findings your centerpiece. Think of your data as a jewel. Your task is to cut and polish it, to select the facets to highlight, and to craft the best setting for it. Many experienced authors write the results section first because it can serve as the outline for the overall story of the article.

But before writing anything, analyze your data!

End of sermonette.

For Whom Should You Write?

Scientific journals are published for specialized audiences who share a common background of substantive knowledge and methodological expertise. If you wish to write well, you should ignore this fact. Psychology encompasses a broader range of subjects and methodologies than do most other disciplines, and its findings are frequently of interest to a wider public. The social psychologist should be able to read a *Psychometrika* article on logistic regression; the personality theorist, a *Science* article on hypothalamic function; and the congressional aide with a BA in history, a *Journal of Personality and Social Psychology* article on attribution theory.

Accordingly, good writing is good teaching. Direct your writing to the student in Psychology 101, your colleague in the Art History Department, and your grandmother. No matter how technical or abstruse your article is in its particulars, intelligent nonpsychologists with no expertise in statistics or experimental design should be able to comprehend the broad outlines of what you did and why. They should understand in general terms what was learned. And above all, they should appreciate why someone – anyone – should give a damn.

The introduction and discussion sections in particular should be accessible to this wider audience.

The actual technical materials – those found primarily in the method and results sections – should be aimed at a reader one level of expertise less specialized than the audience for which the journal is primarily published. Assume that the reader of your article in *Psychometrika* knows about regression, but needs some introduction to logistic regression. Assume that the reader of the *Journal of Personality and Social Psychology* knows about person perception but needs some introduction to dispositional and situational attributions.

Many of the writing techniques suggested in this chapter are thus teaching techniques designed to make your article comprehensible to the widest possible audience. They are also designed to remain invisible or transparent to your readers, thereby infusing your prose with a "subliminal pedagogy." Good writing is good teaching.

WRITING IT

The primary criteria for good scientific writing are accuracy and clarity. If your article is interesting and written with style, fine. But these are subsidiary virtues. First strive for accuracy and clarity.

The first step toward clarity is to write simply and directly. A journal article tells a straightforward tale of a circumscribed problem in search of an answer. It is not a novel with subplots and flashbacks but a short story with a single, linear narrative line. Let this line stand out in bold relief. Clear any underbrush that entangles your prose by obeying Strunk and White's (1979) famous dictum, "omit needless words," and by extending the dictum to needless concepts, topics, anecdotes, asides, and footnotes. If a point seems tangential to your basic argument, remove it. If you can't bring yourself to do this, put it in a footnote. Then, when you revise your manuscript, remove the footnote. In short, don't make your voice struggle to be heard above the ambient noise of cluttered writing. Let your 90th percentile verbal aptitude nourish your prose, not glut it. Write simply and directly.

The second step toward clarity is good organization, and the standardized format of a journal article does much of the work for you. It not only permits readers to read the report from beginning to end, as they would any coherent narrative, but also to scan it for a quick overview of the study or to locate specific information easily by turning directly to the relevant section. Within that format, however, it is still helpful to work from an outline of your own. This enables you to examine the logic of the sequence, spot important points that are omitted or misplaced, and decide how best to divide the narrative between the introduction and final discussion.

An article is written in the shape of an hourglass. It begins with broad general statements, progressively narrows down to the specifics of your study, and then broadens out again to more general considerations. Thus:

> *The introduction begins broadly:* "Individuals differ radically from one another in the degree to which they are willing and able to express their emotions."
>
> *It becomes more specific:* "Indeed, the popular view is that such emotional expressiveness is a central difference between men and women. . . . But the research evidence is mixed..."
>
> *And more so:* "There is even some evidence that men may actually . . ."
>
> *Until you are ready to introduce your own study in conceptual terms:* "In this study, we recorded the emotional reactions of both men and women to filmed . . ."
>
> *The method and results sections are the most specific, the "neck" of the hourglass:* [Method] "One hundred male and 100 female undergraduates were shown one of two movies . . ."
>
> [Results] "Table 1 shows that men in the father-watching condition cried significantly more . . ."
>
> *The discussion section begins with the implications of your study:* "These results imply that sex differences in emotional expressiveness are moderated by two kinds of variables . . ."
>
> *It becomes broader:* "Not since Charles Darwin's first observations has psychology contributed as much new . . ."
>
> *And more so:* "If emotions can incarcerate us by hiding our complexity, at least their expression can liberate us by displaying our authenticity."

This closing statement might be a bit grandiose for some journals – I'm not even sure what it means – but if your study is carefully executed and conservatively interpreted, most editors will permit you to indulge yourself a bit at the two broad ends of the hourglass. Being dull only appears to be a prerequisite for publishing in the professional journals.

REWRITING IT

For many writers revising a manuscript is unmitigated agony. Even proofreading is painful. And so they don't. So relieved to get a draft done, they run it through the spell checker – some don't even do that – and then send it off to the journal, thinking that they can clean up the writing after the article has been accepted. Alas, that day rarely comes. Some may find solace in the belief that the manuscript probably would have been rejected even if it had been extensively revised and polished; after all, most APA journals accept only 15–20% of all manuscripts submitted. But from my own experience as an editor of an APA journal, I believe that the difference between the articles accepted and the top 15–20% of those rejected is frequently the difference between good and less good writing. Moral: Don't expect journal reviewers to discern your brilliance through the smog of polluted writing. Revise your manuscript. Polish it. Proofread it. Then submit it.

Rewriting is difficult for several reasons. First, it is difficult to edit your own writing. You will not notice ambiguities and explanatory gaps because *you* know what you meant to say and *you* understand the omitted steps. One strategy for overcoming this difficulty is to lay your manuscript aside for awhile and then return to it later when it has become less familiar. Sometimes it helps to read it aloud. But there is no substitute for practicing the art of taking the role of the nonspecialist reader, for learning to role-play grandma. As you read, ask yourself, "Have I been told yet what this concept means?" "Has the logic of this step been demonstrated?" "Would I know what the independent variable is at this point?" This is precisely the skill of the good lecturer in Psychology 101: the ability to anticipate the audience's level of understanding at each point in the presentation. Good writing is good teaching.

But because this is not easy, you should probably give a copy of a fairly polished manuscript to a friend or colleague for a critical reading. If you get critiques from several colleagues, you will have simulated the journal's review process. The best readers are those who have themselves had articles published in psychological journals but who are unfamiliar with the subject of your manuscript.

If your colleagues find something unclear, do not argue with them. They are right: By definition, the writing is unclear. Their suggestions for correcting the unclarities may be wrongheaded; but as unclarity detectors, readers are never wrong. Also resist the temptation simply to clarify their confusion verbally. Your colleagues don't want to offend you or appear stupid, so they simply mumble "oh yes, of course, of course" and apologize for not having read carefully enough. As a consequence, you are pacified, and your next readers, the journal's reviewers, will stumble over the same problem. They will not apologize; they will reject.

Rewriting is difficult for a second reason: It requires a high degree of compulsiveness and attention to detail. The probability of writing a sentence perfectly the first time is vanishingly small, and good writers rewrite nearly every sentence of a manuscript in the course of polishing successive drafts. But even good writers differ from one another in their approach to the first draft. Some spend a long time carefully choosing each word and reshaping each sentence and paragraph as they go. Others pound out a rough draft quickly and then go back for extensive revision. Although I personally prefer the former method, I think it wastes time. Most writers should probably get the first draft done as quickly as possible without agonizing over stylistic niceties. Once it is done, however, compulsiveness and attention to detail become the required virtues.

Finally, rewriting is difficult because it usually means restructuring. Sometimes it is necessary to discard whole sections of a manuscript, add new ones, and then totally reorganize the manuscript just to iron out a bump in the logic of the argument. Don't get so attached to your first draft that you are unwilling to tear it apart and rebuild it. (This is why the strategy of crafting each sentence of a first draft wastes time. A beautiful turn of phrase that took me 20 minutes to shape gets discarded when I have to restructure the manuscript. Worse, I get so attached to the phrase that I resist restructuring until

I can find a new home for it.) A badly constructed building cannot be salvaged by brightening up the wallpaper. A badly constructed manuscript cannot be salvaged by changing words, inverting sentences, and shuffling paragraphs.

Which brings me to the word processor. Its very virtuosity at making these cosmetic changes will tempt you to tinker endlessly, encouraging you in the illusion that you are restructuring right there in front of the monitor. Do not be fooled. You are not. A word processor – even one with a fancy outline mode – is not an adequate restructuring tool for most writers. Moreover, it can produce flawless, physically beautiful drafts of wretched writing, encouraging you in the illusion that they are finished manuscripts ready to be submitted. Do not be fooled. They are not. If you are blessed with an excellent memory (or a very large monitor) and are confident that you can get away with a purely electronic process of restructuring, do it. But don't be ashamed to print out a complete draft of your manuscript; spread it out on table or floor; take pencil, scissors, and Scotch tape in hand; and then, all by your low-tech self, have at it.

If, after all this, your manuscript still seems interesting and you still believe the results and interpretation of your study, submit it.

SOME MATTERS OF STYLE

Metacomments

It is often helpful to give readers of an article an early overview of its structure and content. But beyond that, you should avoid making "metacomments" about the writing. Expository prose fails its mission if it diverts the reader's attention to itself and away from the topic; the process of writing should be invisible to the reader. In particular, the prose itself should direct the flow of the narrative without requiring you to play tour guide. Don't say, "Now that the three theories of emotion have been discussed, we can turn to the empirical work on each of them. We begin with the psychoanalytic account of affect. . . ." Instead, move directly from your discussion of the theories into the review of the evidence with a simple transition sentence such as, "Each of these three theories has been tested empirically. Thus, the psychoanalytic account of affect has received support in studies that. . . ." In the results section, don't say: "Now that we have seen the results for negative affect, we are in a position to examine men's and women's emotional expression in the realm of positive affect. The relevant data are presented in Table 2 . . ." Instead use a transition sentence that simultaneously summarizes and moves the story along: "Men may thus be more expressive than women in the domain of negative emotion, but are they also more expressive in the domain of positive emotion? Table 2 shows that they are not . . ." Any other guideposts needed can be supplied by using informative headings and by following the advice on repetition and parallel construction given in the next section.

If you feel the need to make metacomments to keep the reader on the narrative path, then your plot line is probably already too cluttered or pretzel shaped, the writing insufficiently linear. Metacomments only oppress the prose further. Instead, copyedit. Omit needless words, don't add them.

Repetition and Parallel Construction

Inexperienced writers often substitute synonyms for recurring words and vary their sentence structure in the mistaken belief that this is more creative and interesting. Instead of using repetition and parallel construction, as in "women may be more expressive than men in the domain of positive emotion, but they are not more expressive in the domain of negative emotion," they attempt to be more creative: "Women may be more expressive than men in the domain of positive emotion, but it is not the case that they are more prone than the opposite sex to display the less cheerful affects."

Such creativity is hardly more interesting, but it is certainly more confusing. In scientific communication, it can be deadly. When an author uses different words to refer to the same concept in a technical article – where accuracy is paramount – readers justifiably wonder if different meanings are implied. The example in the preceding paragraph is not disastrous, and most readers will be unaware that their understanding flickered momentarily when the prose hit a bump. But consider the cognitive burden carried by readers who must hack through this "creative" jungle:

The low-dissonance participants were paid a large sum of money while not being given a free choice of whether or not to participate, whereas the individuals we randomly assigned to the small-incentive treatment (the high-dissonance condition) were offered the opportunity to refuse.

This (fictitious) writer should have written,

Low-dissonance individuals were paid a large sum of money and were required to participate; high-dissonance individuals were paid a small sum of money and were not required to participate.

The wording and grammatical structure of the two clauses are held rigidly parallel; only the variables vary. Repetition and parallel construction are among the most effective servants of clarity. Don't be creative; be clear.

Repetition and parallel construction also serve clarity at a larger level of organization. By providing the reader with distinctive guideposts to the structure of the prose, they can diminish or eliminate the need for metacomments on the writing. Here, for example, are the opening sentences from three of the paragraphs in the previous section on rewriting:

2nd paragraph: "Rewriting is difficult for several reasons. First . . ."
5th paragraph: "Rewriting is difficult for a second reason."
6th paragraph: "And finally, rewriting is difficult because it . . ."

If I had substituted synonyms for the recurring words or varied the grammatical structure of these opening sentences, their guiding function would have been lost, the reader's sense of the section's organization blurred. (I try so hard to be helpful and I bet you didn't even notice. That, of course, is the point.)

And finally, repetition and parallel construction can serve style and creativity as well as clarity. For example, they can establish metaphor: "A badly constructed building cannot be salvaged by brightening up the wallpaper. A badly constructed article cannot be salvaged by changing words, inverting sentences, and shuffling paragraphs." And, they can add humor: "The word processor encourages you in the illusion that you are restructuring. Do not be fooled. You are not. The word processor encourages you in the illusion that your drafts are finished manuscripts. Do not be fooled. They are not."

Jargon and Technical Terms

The specialized terminology of a discipline is called jargon, and it serves a number of legitimate functions in scientific communication. A specialized term may be more general, more precise, or freer of surplus meaning than any natural language equivalent (e.g., the term *disposition* encompasses, and hence is more general than, beliefs, attitudes, moods, and personality attributes; *reinforcement* is more precise and freer of surplus meaning than *reward*). Also, the technical vocabulary often makes an important conceptual distinction not apprehended in the layperson's lexicon (e.g., genotype vs. phenotype).

But if a jargon term does not satisfy any of these criteria, opt for English. Much of our jargon has become second nature to us and serves only to muddy our prose. (As an editor, I once had to interrogate an author at length to learn that a prison program for "strengthening the executive functions of the ego" actually taught prisoners how to fill out job applications.) And unless the jargon term is extremely well known (e.g., reinforcement), it should be defined – explicitly, implicitly, or by context and example – the first time it is introduced.

For example, in an article on ESP, a coauthor and I decided that we could not proceed beyond the opening paragraph until we had first explicitly defined and clarified the unfamiliar but central theoretical term:

The term *psi* denotes anomalous processes of information or energy transfer, processes such as telepathy or other forms of extrasensory perception that are currently unexplained in terms of known physical or biological mechanisms. The term is purely descriptive: It neither implies that such anomalous phenomena are paranormal nor connotes anything about their underlying mechanisms. (Bem & Honorton, 1994, p. 4)

Here is how one might define a technical term (ego control) and identify its conceptual status (a personality variable) more implicitly:

The need to delay gratification, control impulses, and modulate emotional expression is the earliest and most ubiquitous demand that society places upon the developing child. Because success at so many of life's tasks depends critically on the individual's mastery of such ego control, evidence for life-course continuities in this central personality domain should be readily obtained.

And finally, here is a (made-up) example in which the technical terms are defined only by the context. Note, however, that the technical abbreviation, MAO, is still identified explicitly when it is first introduced.

In the continuing search for the biological correlates of psychiatric disorder, blood platelets are now a prime target of investigation. In particular, reduced monoamine oxidase (MAO) activity in the platelets is sometimes correlated with paranoid symptomatology, auditory hallucinations or delusions in chronic schizophrenia, and a tendency toward psychopathology in normal men. Unfortunately, these observations have not always replicated, casting doubt on the hypothesis that MAO activity is, in fact, a biological marker in psychiatric disorder. Even the general utility of the platelet model as a key to central nervous system abnormalities in schizophrenia remains controversial. The present study attempts to clarify the relation of MAO activity to symptomatology in chronic schizophrenia.

This kind of writing would not appear in *Newsweek*, and yet it is still accessible to a nonspecialist who may never even have heard of blood platelets, MAO activity, or biological markers. The structure of the writing itself adequately defines the relationships among these things and provides enough context to make the basic rationale behind the study comprehensible. At the same time, this introduction is neither condescending nor boring to the technically sophisticated reader. The pedagogy that makes it accessible to the nonspecialist is not only invisible to the specialist but also enhances the clarity of the article for both readers.

Voice and Self-Reference

In the past, scientific writers used the passive voice almost exclusively and referred to themselves in the third person: "This experiment was designed by the investigators to test . . ." This practice produces lifeless prose and is no longer the norm. Use the active voice unless style or content dictates otherwise, and, in general, keep self-reference to a minimum. Remember that you are not the subject of your article. You should not refer to yourself as "the author" or "the investigator." (You may refer to "the experimenter" in the method section, however, even if that happens to be you; the experimenter is part of the subject under discussion there.) You may use the pronoun *we* to refer to yourself and your coauthors, but not to yourself as sole author. In that case, you may refer to yourself as "I", but do so sparingly. It tends to distract the reader from the topic, and it is better to remain in the background. The *Publication Manual* also advises avoiding the use of *we* in broader ways that leave readers uncertain to whom it refers. For example, the sentence beginning with "We usually classify bird song . . ." should be changed to "Researchers usually classify bird song . . ."

Finally, you should leave the reader in the background, too. Don't say, "The reader will find it hard to believe that . . ." or "You will be surprised to learn . . ." (This chapter violates the rule because you and your writing are the subject.) You may, however, occasionally refer to the reader indirectly in imperative, "you-understood" sentences: "Consider, first, the results for women."

BEYOND PUBLICATION

In this book, we have presumed that your pressing pragmatic purpose is to transform your studies into publishable – nay, published – prose. But let your grander goal be to gift that prose with the effortless grace and supple simplicity of a Mozart sonata. This guiding metaphor may not turn all your studies into publications – even Mozart died a pauper – but it will turn even your sow's ears into vinyl purses.

REFERENCES

American Psychological Association. (1994). *Publication manual of the American Psychological Association* (4th ed.). Washington, DC: Author.

Bem, D. J. (1987), Writing the empirical journal article. In M. P. Zanna & J. M. Darley (Eds.), *The compleat academic: A practical guide for the beginning social scientist* (pp. 171–201). New York: Random House.

Bem, D. J. (1995). Writing a review article for *Psychological Bulletin. Psychological Bulletin, 118*, 172–177.

Bem, D. J., & Honorton, C. (1994). Does psi exist? Replicable evidence for an anomalous process of information transfer. *Psychological Bulletin, 115*, 4–18.

Strunk, W., Jr., & White, E. B. (1999). *The elements of style* (4th ed.). New York: Simon & Schuster.

Chapter 2

Writing a Literature Review

NANCY EISENBERG

W riting a literature review requires a somewhat different set of skills than writing an empirical research article. Indeed, some people who are very good at writing empirical research reports are not skilled at composing review papers. What are the characteristics that differentiate literature reviews that are likely to be published and make a difference from those that are difficult to publish and make a limited contribution?

I have been thinking about this topic quite a lot recently. As the current editor of *Psychological Bulletin*, the literature review journal of the American Psychological Association, I constantly deal with the issue of evaluating review papers. I had written a number of literature reviews myself prior to becoming editor; however, in the process of editing the journal I have had to consolidate what were vague, sometimes unverbalized cognitions regarding the properties of an excellent review into criteria for guiding editorial decisions.

Before writing this chapter, I started to outline my recommendations. As a last step before beginning to write, I read a similar paper written by Daryl Bem that was published in *Psychological Bulletin* in 1995. I was surprised at how similar Bem's and my ideas were; sometimes he even used the same words that I have used when talking about writing reviews to groups at conferences and to my students. Based on

Work on this chapter was supported by a grant from the National Institutes of Mental Health (1 R01 HH55052) and a Research Scientist Award from the National Institute of Mental Health (K05 M801321) to Nancy Eisenberg.

this similarity, one could conclude either that great minds think alike or that there is considerable interrater reliability between people who have been editors about what constitutes a high-quality review paper. Although I wish the former explanation for the similarity were true (I admire Bem's writings), the latter is the more likely explanation. In fact, in my experience, even people who occasionally review manuscripts for *Psychological Bulletin* tend to agree on the structural qualities of an acceptable review paper, although they sometimes disagree on the value or veracity of specific content in a given review paper.

In this chapter, I discuss the various types of literature reviews and provide guidelines for writing a high-quality review article. The expectations for, and criteria for acceptance of, review papers in the top journals are, of course, more stringent than those for acceptance in second or third tier journals. Nonetheless, many of the same rules apply for writing a review for a premier journal and for other journals.

THE PURPOSES OF REVIEW ARTICLES

A good starting place for considering the purpose of a review paper is the discussion of review papers in the *Publication Manual of the American Psychological Association* (APA, 1994):

Review articles, including meta-analyses, are critical evaluations of material that has already been published. By organizing, integrating, and evaluating previously published material, the author of a review article considers the progress of current research toward clarifying a problem. In a sense, a review article is tutorial in that the author

- defines and clarifies the problem;
- summarizes previous investigations in order to inform the reader of the state of current research;
- identifies relations, contradictions, gaps, and inconsistencies in the literature; and
- suggests the next step or steps in solving the problem. (1994, p. 5)

In my editorial in *Psychological Bulletin* (1997), I outlined three types of reviews that I expected to publish in the *Bulletin*. I would now add a fourth. The purposes of these types of reviews differ somewhat, although the various types of reviews are not mutually exclusive.

1. In a common type of review, an author uses existing empirical data to answer old or new questions. For example, the author might review studies on age-related changes or sex differences in a given aspect of psychological functioning or behavior and evaluate whether, to what degree, and under what conditions age changes or sex differences seem to occur (e.g., Eagly & Steffen, 1986). A review of this type may be based on quantitative methods such as meta-analytic procedures that combine empirical findings across studies or can be based on the author's qualitative review of the literature. In this type of review, the major contribution generally is the *generation of new knowledge,* although theoretical or conceptual predictions usually are examined, for example, the new knowledge is linked to conceptual frameworks already in existence or formulated in the manuscript.

2. Reviews often are a vehicle for analyzing and evaluating the specific predictions of existing theories or conceptual models. Such a paper may include solely a qualitative review of the literature (i.e., a review that does not involve any statistical computations across studies) and/or quantitative methods for combining results across studies. With meta-analytic procedures, an author can use a set of studies to empirically test theoretical claims and potential moderating variables that qualify when and if a predicted effect or relation is obtained (e.g., Eagly, Chaiken, Chen, & Shaw-Barnes, 1999; Postmes & Spears, 1998). The primary goal of this sort of paper is *theory testing.*

3. Another slightly different type of review is one in which the author integrates and/or compares conceptual frameworks and empirical findings from different subdisciplines or conceptual approaches in psychology or from psychology and other disciplines (e.g., economics, genetics, or anthropological work). For example, an author might evaluate the cognitive developmental conception of children's theories of mind stemming from developmental psychology in light of ethnographic work from anthropology and related disciplines (Lillard, 1998). The primary purposes of this type of review are *theory integration or theory testing.*

4. In some reviews, a new conceptual model is the center point of the paper and an author uses this conceptual model or theoretical prediction to organize a body of literature into meaningful patterns.

As just one example, authors have presented a new model of how people respond to the receipt of aid from others (and the underlying processes), and then used the model as a basis for organizing relevant literature and theory (see Fisher, Nadler, & Witcher-Alagna, 1982, and Shell & Eisenberg, 1992, for examples). Another example is Bjorklund's (1997) review in which he proposed a somewhat novel prediction based on evolutionary theory (i.e., that infants' and young children's immature behaviors and cognitions sometimes are adaptive) and organized his review around examining the merit of this proposal. The primary goal of reviews of this type is to *develop and evaluate new theory or conceptual arguments.*

The four types of reviews listed above do not include the most common type of review published in the psychological literature. A fifth type of literature review involves the organization, presentation, and summarization of preexisting theory and empirical findings. There is limited, if any, generation of new knowledge or theory. For example, if a field is new, an author might review what is known in an effort to organize and consolidate a sparse or scattered database so that one can more easily draw conclusions and provide direction for future research. The primary purpose of these types of reviews is the *integration and presentation of existing knowledge.*

There are also many other kinds of reviews, such as those in which authors evaluate the usefulness of a particular measure, trace the history of a given concept or type of research, or provide information on how to use specific clinical, intervention, or laboratory procedures. Reviews such as these generally, but not always, are published in books aimed at a specific, fairly specialized audience.

SELECTING A JOURNAL

Whether a literature review is likely to be accepted by a high-quality, peer-reviewed journal depends, in part, on the type of review and its appropriateness for a given journal. Literature reviews that organize and summarize an existing body of literature or spell out how to use various measures or procedures certainly have a useful place in psychology. Such reviews educate people without specific expertise in an area, are helpful to readers who want to cite a summary of the current state of knowledge in an area, and provide a jumping off point for researchers who want to move beyond the current state of empirical knowledge. However, reviews that merely summarize current knowledge generally are most appropriate for books or perhaps a special issue of a specialty journal on the specific topic. Although they sometimes may be published in some journals, they currently are not common in the premier psychological journals. Review articles that are most likely to be accepted in peer-reviewed review journals are those in which authors generate new knowledge, generate or evaluate theory (broadly defined), and/or integrate ideas and findings from different disciplines in a new way. In brief, top quality reviews are expected to provide a novel contribution of some sort and to deal with conceptual issues.

In my experience, it is relatively easy to write a review that merely summarizes existing knowledge. In contrast, writing a review that is conceptually based and provides a novel contribution is much more difficult. Doing so usually requires that your thinking about the topic of the paper has "jelled," which generally occurs only after being immersed in a domain of study for some period of time. A review that provides an increment in knowledge or theory also requires a bit of inspiration. Of course, you can compute a meta-analysis on some issue without broaching new conceptual territory – and such a meta-analysis may generate new knowledge – but the review is likely to be a bit hollow, sterile, and uninspired if you have not reflected extensively on the topic. There is no substitute for a thoughtful and creative analysis of a domain, even if a review paper includes an empirical meta-analysis.

Not all journals that publish reviews require that articles extend the boundaries of our knowledge and thinking. As noted previously, a solid, comprehensive review, especially if carefully conducted, is acceptable in some peer-reviewed journals. A good way to evaluate the fit between your review and a specific journal is to examine reviews previously published in that journal to see if their contribution is similar to that in your manuscript.

In an analysis of the degree to which ratings of criteria similar to those just discussed predicted acceptance of manuscripts in

Psychological Bulletin in 1993–1996, Sternberg, Hojjat, Brigockas, and Grigorenko (1997) found that all ratings predicted final decisions, that the ratings were highly intercorrelated, and that the two strongest predictors were contribution to the field reviewed and appropriateness of manuscript for the journal. Thus, it is important to consider the degree and type of contribution of a review paper, as well as its appropriateness for a given journal, when evaluating if a manuscript is likely to be published in a peer-reviewed journal. Moreover, the breadth of the topic should be taken into account. If your topic is of interest to a narrow audience of psychologists, it probably is more appropriate for a specialty journal in a given discipline (e.g., *Personality and Social Psychology Review, Human Development,* or *Developmental Review*) than for a journal targeted at a broad audience (e.g., *Psychological Bulletin*). Choosing the appropriate journal for submission can save you from losing many months in the review process, time that is particularly valuable if the content of a paper is likely to become dated.

COMMON PROBLEMS IN THE CONTENT OF REVIEW PAPERS

Your odds of writing a publishable review are increased if you are aware of what editors and reviewers expect in the content of reviews. One of the best ways to get a feel for this is to read reviews in top-notch journals and in the journal to which you plan to submit your manuscript (if they are not the same). Below I outline some important points to keep in mind when organizing and writing your review article.

Provide a Take-Home Message

As noted by Sternberg (1991), the past editor of *Psychological Bulletin,* a central ingredient of a top-notch review paper (and hopefully an ingredient in any review article) is a "take-home message."

Literature reviews are often frustrating because they offer neither a point of view nor a take-home message. One is left with a somewhat undigested scattering of facts but little with which to put them together. (p.3)

Stated somewhat differently,

Authors of literature reviews are at risk for producing mind-numbing lists of citations and findings that resemble a phone book—impressive cast, lots of numbers, but not much plot. (Bem, 1995, p. 172)

In brief, reviews should have a point that a reader can take away from the paper. Of course, that point needs to be clear and well justified if the paper is to be convincing. You are more likely to present a clear message if the central message is adequately introduced in the introduction and if you provide readers with a conceptual framework early in the paper that can be used to assimilate and integrate the review of empirical evidence that follows the introduction. By providing a conceptual framework and/or guideposts (i.e., advanced organizers) for readers early in the paper, you help the reader to see things from your perspective.

The Review of the Empirical Literature

There are several issues that arise regarding the quality of the section of the paper that includes the actual review of the existing empirical literature.

Breadth of the Review. The breadth of desirable coverage of the empirical literature (or theory) varies with the purpose of the literature review. If you are attempting to evaluate the pattern of findings for the body of research on a particular issue, it is important that the review be inclusive. Most or much of the relevant empirical work, especially research of high quality, should be discussed. Bodies of research using diverse methods usually should be included (unless an author is focusing on a particular method), and the range of findings should be reported. Of utmost importance, the review should not be biased in coverage toward research supporting your point of view by excluding empirical work inconsistent with your perspective. A biased review is of little use to the discipline and is poor science.

There are cases in which the review of particular parts of the empirical literature would be expected to be more selective, albeit still representative. For example, if you are presenting a broad model and need to illustrate one of many points related to part of the model, an in-depth review of the literature may be unnecessary and could be distracting. Nonetheless, if you cite a small subset of studies, this subset of research should represent the best work available and you should note discrepancies across studies that are relevant to your argument.

Thus far I have been discussing breadth of coverage in terms of the range and number of studies included in the review. A related issue is the level of detail provided about particular studies or bodies of research. An inclusive literature review does not require that you discuss every study in detail. Often bodies of research can be summarized in a few sentences, especially if the methods used are similar across studies. If presentation of details is deemed important, findings and characteristics of the sample and design can be summarized for specific studies in a table that is available for the reader's perusal. A long discussion of the characteristics and findings of many individual studies is desirable only when it is necessary to make a point, such as why findings differ across studies.

Nonetheless, you do not want your paper to have a "trust me" feel to it. In general, the reader should have some idea of the methods used in the work and the nature of the empirical evidence (e.g., Are the data correlational or from an experimental design? Do the studies involve cross-sectional or longitudinal samples? What types of families tended to be involved in the research?). Often you can provide the essential information very briefly. The degree to which such detail is necessary depends, of course, on the centrality of the study or studies to the point you wish to make.

Relevance. Often authors review theory or research that is not central to their premise or focus. They get off on a mental tangent that serves only to confuse the reader. The content of your review should be on *relevant* literature and pertinent points; otherwise, the logic of your argument or analysis gets lost. I return to the issue of logic of the argument shortly.

Accuracy. It is a problem if the content in a review of the literature is incorrect or misleading. In addition to a review being biased based on the selection of studies, authors sometimes misrepresent the results of studies or the views of a theorist. Sometimes these misrepresentations are based on an honest difference in individuals' interpretations or understanding of data or theory. However, often misrepresentations are due to careless reading and reporting of find-ings. In addition, sometimes an author knowingly slants the findings in a particular direction by omitting relevant information. It is not a problem to differ in your interpretation of findings from other researchers or authors – indeed, having a novel point of view can be the contribution of your paper. But when this is the case, it is wise to lay out carefully your reasons for interpreting the findings as you do. If an author ignores or simply dismisses others' interpretations of the literature without sufficient cause or misstates others' views to make a point, he or she eventually will be seen as an advocate of a particu-lar perspective, not as a scientist.

Another component of accuracy is being sure that the conclu-sions you present as stemming from your review of the literature actually do follow from the review. Often authors make assertions following their discussion of the literature that are not really sub-stantiated by the material reviewed. Of course, it is reasonable (and even desirable) for you to go beyond the work reviewed and to spec-ulate about relevant issues, mechanisms, processes, and the like. However, it should be clear to the reader what is speculation not grounded in the literature review and what conclusions are firmly based on your review of studies.

Inclusion of Critique. A strong review paper is written from a critical point of view. The author does not simply accept what is out there in the existing literature; he or she evaluates the methods of studies, other authors' conclusions, and other aspects of relevant the-ory or research that are relevant to evaluating a body of work. A criti-cal evaluation of relevant work includes pointing out strengths as well as weaknesses in existing research and theory. Taking a critical per-spective does not mean that you must tear apart every study. Criticism usually is most helpful if you provide an assessment of the strengths and weaknesses of a body of work, including the evidence for specific points or conclusions. For example, you can point out the strengths and weaknesses of various methods (e.g., self-reports, experimental manipulations), as well as note when findings converge across methods (and, thus, are likely to be more reliable).

Being critical does not mean being nasty or insulting. Your critical remarks should be focused on the work itself rather than on the researcher or author of that work. *Ad hominem* criticism in manuscripts (or from reviewers) usually is not welcomed by editors or readers and is deemed inappropriate and nonconstructive. Moreover, as was pragmatically noted by Bem (1995), the person you attack is likely to be asked to review your manuscript!

The Ending. The concluding section of a review can be especially useful to readers if you go beyond merely summarizing the findings from the review. This includes not only noting gaps in the literature, unanswered questions, and future directions for research, but also drawing novel conclusions (if justified or plausible), proposing alternative explanations or processes to explain findings, and discussing the implications of your findings for theory. Authors generally are given more latitude when discussing the findings of a review of the literature than when discussing the results of an empirical paper based on one study or a series of studies. Thus, review papers provide an opportunity for you to be creative and present your own interpretations and integration of the literature, even if your thoughts go somewhat beyond the information directly provided by the review. Creativity is a valuable commodity and can enhance the contribution of your manuscript.

QUALITY OF WRITING

A good idea is not enough to get a review accepted – you must present your ideas clearly. Many an article is rejected due to poor writing rather than to lack of a good idea (or good data, for that matter, if you are submitting to an empirical journal). I agree with Bem (1995) that the difference between articles that are accepted and the top 15–20% of those rejected frequently is the quality of writing. Of course, clarity of writing will not substitute for a careful review of the literature and creative thinking. However, clarity of writing allows the reader to extract and appreciate the author's creative, analytical, and integrative contributions.

Organization

I often tell my students that when they write a paper, they need to tell a coherent story (also see Bem, 1995). The logic should be linear: Point A→ point B→ point C. As noted by Bem (1995), "a coherent review emerges only from a coherent conceptual structuring of the topic itself (p. 173)."

As noted by others (Bem, 1995; Sternberg, 1991), no single organization works best for all reviews. One of the best approaches is to organize a review around competing models or around evaluation of a point of view (see Bem, 1995, for examples), but this structure may not work for all content areas. Regardless of the content, you should organize the paper around the central point and the relation of theory and research to this central issue.

I sometimes characterize specific manuscripts as "being written like an undergraduate paper." I am referring to instances in which authors organize their reviews by studies rather than by ideas. One study after another is described, often in too much detail. Studies should not be the unit of analysis; important points to be made should be the building blocks of a review. For example, if an author wants to analyze gender differences in empathy-related responding, the review might be organized according to an analysis of bodies of work pertaining to different conceptualizations of empathy and different operationalizations of empathy-related responding (e.g., self-reports, physiological measures). Then individual studies could be discussed in the context of providing information about particular conceptualizations or operationalizations of the construct.

Take the Perspective of the Reader

Many of the common problems of communication in psychological papers could be corrected if authors simply tried to take the perspective of their readers. Often authors use pronouns (e.g., his or it) when the referent for the pronoun is unclear. Similarly, authors frequently use terms such as "more" or "less" that imply a comparison, but do not indicate what is being compared with what. Consider the sentence, "Aggressive boys were less liked by their peers whereas aggressive girls were more ignored." In this sentence, it is unclear if aggressive boys were less liked by their peers than were less aggressive boys or aggressive girls, and if aggressive girls were more ignored than aggressive boys or nonaggressive girls. Another instance of lack of perspective taking is when authors jump from one idea to the next without an adequate transition or linkage between the two ideas.

When writing any paper, you should actively analyze how a naive reader will interpret what you are saying and where readers will be confused. Readers do not carry the same fund of knowledge in their heads as you do and are not privy to your train of thought. If reviewers or readers are frustrated by unclear references and leaps in logic, they are unlikely to take the energy to read the paper carefully, will miss important points, and may even give up trying to read the paper.

Use Clear Language

There are many ways to improve the clarity of your writing. One is to learn the basics of good writing and grammar that are essential for writing at all levels, professional and otherwise. There are numerous books written on clarity of prose and grammar that are useful guides (e.g., Strunk & White, 1979).

One especially common problem in academic writing is that people tend to use complex phrases and word constructions in their writing. I always tell students to write in the same way that they would explain an idea or findings to an intelligent layperson who does not know the work. I also suggest that they write in a manner similar to how they talk. Most people would never say the things they write; the word constructions in their writing are too convoluted and drawn out. As advised by Bem (1995), "write simply and directly" (p. 173).

Bem (1995) provided a number of examples of concise versus inconcise language, repetitive and parallel constructions in sentences, and concise versus inconcise summarizing of a study. I would like to emphasize one particular problem (also see Bem, 1995) – the use of jargon. Jargon is specialized terminology used in a discipline. Even in the premier journals in psychology, which are read primarily by other psychologists, the use of unnecessary jargon is confusing and undesirable. The content of a review is expected to be accessible to other people not working in precisely the same area as you, and jargon often undermines readers' understanding of critical concepts.

Unless jargon is extremely well known (e.g., "reinforcement"), is more precise or freer of surplus meaning than other terms, or has a specific meaning that is not available in everyday English, it is best to use plain and simple English (Bem, 1995). If you must use jargon, you should define the terms the first time they are presented in the text.

META-ANALYSES

Many reviewers use meta-analytic techniques to combine the results of multiple studies. This can be a very effective procedure for testing empirical questions when sufficient studies exist on the given topic. Meta-analytic procedures are very useful for testing main effects and moderating (i.e., statistical interaction) effects that are hypothesized in models.

The statistical procedures for computing a meta-analysis have been discussed in detail elsewhere (e.g., Cooper & Hedges, 1994; Hedges & Olkin, 1985), as have the components of a meta-analysis (Rosenthal, 1995). I wish only to point out a few of the common errors that I have seen in meta-analytic reviews.

One common error is an author assuming that the meta-analytic section of the paper eliminates the need for a thoughtful introduction section, analytic thinking, and discussion of conceptual issues. The author primarily presents the results of the analysis and assumes that says it all. The inclusion of meta-analyses does not eliminate the need for conceptual integration. Moreover, some relevant data often are not available in a form that can be used in a meta-analysis; research of this type should be reviewed qualitatively if it is pertinent.

Second, a meta-analysis is only as good as the data set of studies used in it. Thus, if you undertake a meta-analysis, your search procedures for obtaining relevant papers should be inclusive, and usually you should include unpublished papers such as dissertations and conference papers (to avoid the problem of bias toward studies in which the results are significant). Moreover, you should describe your search procedures in detail, including what keywords were used in the computer search and what search programs were used (e.g., MedLine, PsychLit).

If you conduct a meta-analysis, there are many decisions you must make regarding aggregation of data from individual studies, the selection of statistics, and so forth. The procedures chosen should be clearly described and, if they are not normative, justified. Moreover, in most cases, it is important that you use the typical range of statistics suggested by experts in meta-analysis (e.g., confidence intervals, estimates of homogeneity of a group of studies).

The important point to keep in mind is that meta-analysis is merely a statistical tool. Thus, the other requirements for a good review generally hold. In addition, the same care that is expected for reporting analyses in empirical articles is applicable to the reporting of meta-analytic procedures and results.

REVISING

Once your draft of an article is finished, it is unlikely to be ready to send off for review. I usually revise and write at least four or five versions of an article before sending it off for review, and additional versions when I am revising after feedback from editors and reviewers. Virtually no papers are accepted at the premier journals without revision. However, you substantially decrease your chances of being allowed to revise if the original draft of the manuscript is poorly written and if there are many grammatical and typographical errors.

In rewriting a paper, most of us need to spend considerable time and energy working on issues such as clarity of wording, clarity of presentation of ideas, and organization of ideas. Often what is needed is some distance from the paper. After you have read and reread the same paper many times, you know the paper so well that it is difficult to note missing words or links between ideas. Putting the paper aside for a few days or weeks and then coming back to it can provide you with a whole new perspective. It also is very useful to ask co-workers to read the manuscript and provide feedback prior to submitting the paper. Ideally, one reader would be familiar with your content area and could comment on content-related issues whereas another reader would be someone without expertise in your particular content area who could provide feedback on clarity of communication in the paper. After more than 20 years of publishing, I still never submit an empirical paper or a major review paper without having at least one other person read it (and usually more than one).

Extensive rewriting, if combined with high quality in terms of content, may earn you a reject–revise review. If the editor leaves the door open for a revision, this generally is cause for guarded celebration; the odds of the paper being accepted have gone up substantially. This is especially true if you think that you can address most of the important issues in the reviews and can provide good reasons for not complying with the suggestions that you do not want to incorporate into the revision. As suggested by Bem (1995), "turn to the task of revising your manuscript with a dispassionate, problem-solving approach" (pp. 176–177). Do whatever seems reasonable (and perhaps slightly unreasonable) to respond to the reviewers' and editors' concerns. Keep in mind that reviewers generally are experts in an area and that many of their comments likely have merit.

You should, of course, feel free to argue, in a constructive way, about any suggestion by an editor or reviewer that you feel is wrong or unwarranted. However, it is wise not to simply ignore suggestions rather than discuss why the suggestions are problematic. It is a good policy to include a letter with your resubmitted manuscript in which you outline in some detail how you handled the reviewers' suggestions and your reasons for not making some suggested modifications. Indeed, many editors request a letter of this sort.

When writing this letter to the editor, keep in mind that reviewers as well as the editor are likely to read it. Original reviewers usually are asked to re-review revised manuscripts, especially if they had criticisms of the manuscript. Thus, it is in your own best interest to bite your tongue when writing this letter and not detail why a reviewer's comments are stupid, just plain wrong, or biased. Reviewers are people, and they often get defensive or downright mad if they are embarrassed or insulted by an author's letter. Your goal should be to have your manuscript re-reviewed by a dispassionate, rational reviewer rather than by a defensive or angered reviewer.

So, for example, when you get the silly suggestion that you reanalyze your correlational data controlling for age when age was not related to any variables in your correlations, vent with your friends or colleagues and then do the correlations. Do not say: "I did not reanalyze controlling for age because the reviewer obviously did not read my paper well enough to note that age was unrelated to any of the variables in the correlations." Rather, you might say. "As suggested by a reviewer, I reanalyzed controlling for age and it had no effect on the results." And perhaps, if you feel other readers might wonder about the same issue, you might add, "and I now mention this fact briefly in a footnote."

When a reviewer suggests that you discuss an issue that is tangential to your point, you shouldn't say, "This reviewer obviously doesn't know the area because he/she suggested I discuss work that is not relevant." Rather, you might say something like the following: "Although the work on topic X is interesting, it is not directly relevant to the point I hope to make. Thus, I simply have briefly cited that body of work so interested readers can access that work. If this is not satisfactory, please let me know." (See Bem, 1995, for other examples of right and wrong responses.)

Persistence, hard work, self-regulation, and a strong ego are important in getting you through the review process. Don't give up on revising your review simply because it is a frustrating, difficult, and time-consuming process or because you are angered by the reviews. Keep in mind the slogan of the Arizona lottery, "You can't win if you don't play."

SUMMARY

As I noted in my editorial outlining the types of papers I hoped to publish in *Psychological Bulletin* (Eisenberg, 1997):

The best reviews are those that provide readers with a well-articulated message and a framework for the integration of information. In addition, reviews are expected to be well organized, comprehensive, critical, and balanced and to communicate clearly to a broad audience. Moreover, a high-quality review identifies relations, gaps, and inconsistencies in the literature and includes ideas regarding the next steps for a solution to the problem. (p. 3)

This is not mere verbiage; I try to carry through on these ideas in the review process. To assess the aforementioned qualities (and others) in papers submitted to *Psychological Bulletin*, I ask reviewers of manuscripts to rate on a five-point scale (from low to high) all manuscripts on the following criteria: (1) significance of paper topic, (2) interest to a broad audience of psychologists, (3) appropriateness for the *Bulletin*, (4) quality of analyses (e.g., meta-analysis; respond only if relevant); (5) balance and fairness in coverage of alternative views, (6) accuracy of information, (7) adequacy of literature review (was the literature adequately sampled?), (8) theoretical contribution of manuscript, (9) existence of and persuasiveness in arguing for a well-articulated point of view, (10) importance of conclusions, (11) quality of writing (clarity, coherence, and organization of the prose), (12) appropriateness of the paper's length (is it concise?), and (13) overall evaluation. Some of these criteria may not apply to some other journals or may not be explicitly assessed by other editors (for example, a review published in a specialty journal need not interest a broad audience of psychologists). Nonetheless, many of these criteria doubtlessly are used to evaluate reviews in most peer-reviewed journals. Contribution to the field is the bottom line, but that contribution is likely to be obscured if your writing is not well organized and clear.

REFERENCES

American Psychological Association. (1994). *Publication manual of the American Psychological Association* (4th ed.). Washington, DC: Author.

Bem, D. J. (1995). Writing a review article for *Psychological Bulletin. Psychological Bulletin, 118*, 172–177.

Bjorklund, D. G. (1997). The role of immaturity in human development. *Psychological Bulletin, 122*, 153–169.

Cooper, H., & Hedges, L. V. (1994). *The handbook of research synthesis.* New York: Russell Sage Foundation.

Eagly A., Chaiken, S., Chen, S., & Shaw-Barnes, K. (1999). The impact of attitudes on memory: An affair to remember. *Psychological Bulletin, 125*, 64–89.

Eagly, A. H., & Steffen, V. J. (1986). Gender and aggressive behavior: A meta-analytic review of the social psychological literature. *Psychological Bulletin, 100*, 309–330.

Eisenberg, N. (1997). Editorial. *Psychological Bulletin, 122*, 3–4.

Fisher, J. D., Nadler, A., & Witcher-Alagna, S. (1982). Recipient reactions to aid. *Psychological Bulletin, 91*, 27–54.

Hedges, L. V., & Olkin, I. (1985). *Statistical methods for meta-analysis.* New York: Academic Press.

Lillard, A. (1998). Ethnopsychologies: Cultural variations in theories of mind. *Psychological Bulletin, 123*, 3–32.

Postmes, T., & Spears, R. (1998). Deindividuation and antinormative behavior: A meta-analytic review. *Psychological Bulletin, 123*, 238–259.

Rosenthal, R. (1995). Writing meta-analytic reviews. *Psychological Bulletin, 118*, 183–192.

Shell, R., & Eisenberg, N. (1992). A developmental model of recipients' reactions
    to aid. *Psychological Bulletin, 111,* 413–433.
Sternberg, R. J. (1991). Editorial. *Psychological Bulletin, 109,* 3–4.
Sternberg, R. J., Hojjat, M., Brigockas, M. G., & Grigorenko, E. L. (1997). Getting
    in: Criteria for acceptance of manuscripts in *Psychological Bulletin,* 1993–1996.
    Psychological Bulletin, 121, 321–323.
Strunk, W., & White, E. B. (1979). *Elements of style* (3rd ed.). New York:
    Macmillan.

PART TWO

PARTS OF AN ARTICLE

Chapter 3

Titles and Abstracts

They Only Sound Unimportant

ROBERT J. STERNBERG

What could be more boring than titles and abstracts, or than an article entitled "Titles and Abstracts"? Yet few aspects of the article are more important than, you guessed it, titles and abstracts. Let's stop being abstract and get concrete. Why are they so important?

1. *Capturing attention.* I sometimes tell my students that, when you write, you have a minute or two, rarely longer, to capture a reader's attention. Either they are with you after that minute or two, or they are gone or not paying attention. As readers start with the title and typically proceed to the abstract, much of the minute or two and sometimes all of it are spent on these opening lines. If the title does not capture interest, readers are unlikely to proceed any further. Often readers scan a table of contents and decide whether the title justifies their even turning to the article. If it does not, you lose your reader. If readers make it to the actual article, often they then decide whether to proceed on the basis of the abstract. If the abstract does not interest them, they read no further. Whether your article will be read by many people, few people, or virtually none at all thus can be largely a function of the title and the abstract.
2. *Databases.* The two aspects of the article most likely to be archived in databases are the title and the abstract. Posterity will judge whether your article is relevant to them largely on the basis of the title and the abstract.

3. *Summaries.* Many people who scan journals, databases, or a journal such as *Current Contents* (which lists nothing more than the tables of contents of various journals) will never see any more than these two elements. Their goal is to get an overview of what you did. You thus want to make the title and abstract as strong as you can.

4. *First impressions.* The title and the abstract give a first impression of you. Are you an interesting thinker or a dull one? Are you an engaging writer or a boring one? When George Miller (1956) entitled an article, "The Magical Number Seven, Plus or Minus Two: Some Limits on our Capacity for Processing Information," he knew exactly what he was doing. He had the reader's interest before the reader even started reading the article proper. He made a great first impression with his title, and even today, the name sticks. How much less of an impact the article might have had if Miller had crafted a pedestrian title like "Limitations on Information-Processing Capacity: A Review of the Literature."

Given the importance of the title and the abstract, what can you do to make them as effective as possible? Consider first titles, then abstracts.

TITLES

The title should inform the reader simply and concisely what the paper is about (*Publication Manual of the American Psychological Association,* 4th ed., APA, 1994; Sternberg, 1993). It is important that the title be self-explanatory. Readers will come across the title in other articles that refer to your own article and in PsychInfo, and they may have to decide whether to read your article solely on the basis of the title. The title should include keywords, for example, the theoretical issue to which the paper is addressed, and possibly the dependent variable(s), and the independent variable(s). Keywords are important because the title will be stored in information-retrieval networks that rely on such words to determine the relevance of your study to someone else's research interests. For the same reason, it is important to avoid irrelevant and misleading words, because such words may spuriously lead an investigator uninterested in your topic to your article. The title typically should not exceed 12–15 words in length.

Everyone has his or her own style in titles, but certain titles take a form that I personally find trite. An example of such a style is "The Effect of—upon —." That may be in fact what you are studying, but the title is boring and the work sounds empirical without any driving theory. Other hackneyed forms for empirical articles are "A Study of —," "An Investigation of —," and "An Experiment on —" Such titles are also redundant, because what else is an empirical article if it is not a study, an investigation, or an experiment? If you are using a theory to drive empirical work, it helps to let this fact be known through your title.

THE ABSTRACT

The abstract summarizes your article (Sternberg, 1993). Its length typically should be 100–150 words for a report of an empirical study, and 75–100 words for a theoretical article or literature review. The abstract, like the title, should be self-explanatory and self-contained because it may be used by information-retrieval networks for indexing.

For empirical articles, the abstract should include (a) the problem being investigated, (b) the major hypotheses, (c) a summary of the method, including a description of the materials, apparatus, participants (including number, sex, and age of participants), design, and procedure, (d) a synopsis of the main results, including significance levels, and (e) the conclusions drawn from the results, as well as any implications of these conclusions. For theoretical and review articles, the abstract should include (a) the problem being studied, (b) the purpose, thesis, or organizing construct, (c) the scope of the analysis, (d) the types of sources used, and (e) the conclusions. Do not include in the abstract any information that is not included in the body of the article. Because you will not know until you are done with the outline what information you will include, you are well advised to defer writing the abstract until after you have otherwise completed the outline or even the whole article.

The APA *Publication Manual* lists several features of a good abstract. These features are that the abstract be (a) accurate, (b) self-contained, (c) concise and specific, (d) nonevaluative, and (e) coherent and readable. Remember that most people will read your abstract only if your title interests them, and will read your article only if your abstract interests them. It is therefore essential that the abstract be interesting. You can interest the reader by showing that the problem is an important one, that your hypotheses about the problem are insightful ones, and that you will test these hypotheses in a convincing way.

REFERENCES

American Psychological Association. (1994). *Publication Manual of the American Psychological Association* (4th ed.) Washington, DC: Author.

Miller, G. (1956). The magical number seven, plus or minus two: Some limits on our capacity for processing information. *Psychological Review, 63*, 81–97.

Sternberg, R. J. (1993). *The psychologist's companion* (3rd ed.). New York: Cambridge University Press.

Chapter 4

Introducing Your Research Report

Writing the Introduction

PHILIP C. KENDALL, JENNIFER S. SILK,
AND BRIAN C. CHU

D rafting an introduction may feel like a daunting task. The
writer must engage the audience in his or her research, provide the necessary background information about the topic, and set
the stage for the study itself. How is this accomplished? First and
foremost, there is no one formula. Consider the following. As undergraduates prepare to apply to graduate school they often ask faculty,
"What makes a successful application?" The applicants invariably
think in a formulaic fashion, believing that a secret formula exists –
something akin to four parts research, two parts practical experience,
GREs over a cutoff score, and an undergraduate GPA of at least 3.5.
They believe that adherence to the recipe will fashion the ideal candidate. Sorry, there is no rigid formula. In fact, whereas the ingredients
of the formula are indeed important to the evaluation process, different schools look differently at the varying credentials.

Likewise, journal editors and readers alike expect the introduction
section of an article to contain certain features, but again there is no
formula. The components of the introduction fit within a general
framework that allows the researcher to describe the study and to
provide a rationale for its implementation. The framework of the
introduction consists of three segments – unequal in length but each
essential in conveying the background and purpose of the study. The
first segment, often the opening paragraph, sets the broad stage for
the research and draws the reader's interest. The second segment provides a focused exposition of the relevant background and provides
support for the decision to do the present study. After laying the

groundwork, the third segment of the introduction provides a transition from past research to the current study, including an explanation of how the study contributes to the research on the topic, the hypothesis for the study, and a brief description of the study's major elements.

Although these three segments constitute the basic structure of the introduction, the manner in which they are crafted varies depending on the specific purpose of the study. If the study is intended to make a striking break from past research, the tone of the writing may be argumentative and the literature review may be used to point out the flaws and limitations of previous studies. If the study is a natural extension or follow-up of previous research, the literature review may simply describe the development of the ideas studied. When the author is trying to draw attention to an often ignored area of research, he or she may attempt to demonstrate its importance to the field and make use of analogies to draw comparisons with other domains of research. Creativity and flexibility within this broad general framework can help convey the importance and necessity of the study and capture the reader's interest and attention.

SECTION I: THE OPENING

The opening segment serves the dual purpose of appealing to the reader's interests and providing a general theoretical and historical framework for the project. The main goal of the segment is to introduce the topic of your investigation so that the reader will be interested in your study and so that he or she will be able to place the more detailed research review into a larger context.

The first paragraph offers some appeal to the reader. The initial statements may be treated as if the author were talking to someone outside the specific area of research and wanted to draw his or her interest in reading the paper. Several tactics are commonly employed to engage the reader's interest in the first few sentences of the opening segment (see "Strategies for the Opening Paragraph"). Techniques often found in journal articles include rhetorical questions, analogies, striking statistics or facts, brief historical summaries of the topic, definitions, or everyday examples of a phenomenon. Consider the fol-

---

STRATEGIES FOR THE OPENING PARAGRAPH

- *Rhetorical Question:* Opening with a rhetorical question automatically engages the reader, sets him or her in the right framework, and personalizes it. The question prompts the reader to ask, "What do I think about this subject?"
- *Everyday Experience:* The author can demonstrate the relevance of the research topic by comparing it to a common experience.
- *Analogy/Metaphor:* Providing the reader with an analogy serves to broaden the scope of the topic, addressing general principles while framing the topic in a familiar arena.
- *Striking Statistic/Fact:* Using an unusual fact compels the reader to rethink his or her views about the subject. The fact conveys the gravity of the topic and the ramifications of future study.
- *Historical Fact:* At times, it can be useful to lay out a brief historical background of the problem. This procedure may be used primarily in expository articles where the primary purpose is to describe the development of the domain of research over time. Historical facts also provide a historical context within which to place the current study.
- *Lack of Previous Research:* By citing the paucity of previous research, the author conveys the sense of importance of the further study.

---

lowing examples of opening statements drawn from research published in American Psychological Association (APA) journals.

The following opening paragraph is from a study published in the *Journal of Consulting and Clinical Psychology* that examined the nature of differences among people in their experience of personal anxious arousal on behalf of another person in a distressing situation (Kendall, Finch, & Montgomery, 1978):

Imagine an evening "on the town" in which an audience is exposed to a theatrical misfortune—an unprepared understudy. As anyone who has been in such a situation knows, there will be large differences in the behavior of the ticket holders. Some will demand a refund, whereas others will feel sorry and work themselves into an anxious sweat! What are the relevant personality characteristics and cognitive reappraisal styles that are associated with such response variation? (p. 997)

This study used an *everyday experience* to demonstrate to the reader the relevance of the research question. By opening with a scenario that any reader could relate to, the introduction attracts the attention of a wide audience. By providing a "leading scenario" that some may have experienced, the authors lead the reader to ask the same question that they eventually propose – that is, why might people differ in their responses to such a situation?

This introduction also makes use of another tactic, the *rhetorical question*, which automatically forces the reader to become an active participant because he or she must "answer" the question before reading further. The reader is compelled to form his or her opinion first, and then is in the position to agree or disagree with the previous research or the author's opinion. Notice that the question is targeted at a specific variable or construct. The authors do not ask the more general question, "Why do people react this way?" Instead, the authors use the rhetorical question to focus the reader's attention on a particular "cognitive reappraisal style" so that the reader will know the study's precise aim.

The use of a rhetorical question and an everyday experience was also illustrated in the introduction to an article in the *Journal of Experimental Psychology: General* about the anchoring effect, a heuristic studied in social psychology (Wilson, Houston, Etling, & Brekke, 1996):

How many physicians practice medicine in your community? Suppose that before answering this question you had just written down the street address of a friend, which happened to be 3459. Would the street address influence your answer to the question about the number of physicians? Would your estimate be higher than if your friend's address happened to be 63? The purpose of this article is to explore the nature of anchoring effects such as this hypothetical one whereby an arbitrary number in memory influences an unrelated judgment. (p. 387)

This introduction draws the attention of any reader – even one who has no idea what the "anchoring heuristic" might be – and leaves the reader curious to find out more about the study. This is accomplished by asking the reader a question and by placing the research topic in a framework that is readily understandable and relevant to everyday life.

Another common strategy used to engage interest is establishing the need for research on a particular topic. This approach is often accomplished by opening with a *striking fact or statistic* that will impress upon the reader the prevalence or magnitude of a particular problem or issue. Although striking statistics are often very effective in catching a reader's eye, the writer should be careful not to overload the introductory segment with numbers. Consider, for example, the striking effect of this introductory paragraph from an article published in *Psychological Assessment* about an assessment system for classifying female prison inmates (Megargee, 1997):

From 1973 through 1993, the number of people incarcerated in state and federal prisons in the United States increased 446%. During that period the rate of increase among female offenders (846%) was almost twice that of their male counterparts (435%; Meguire & Pastore, 1995). (p. 75).

Another way of establishing the need for a study is by pointing to a *lack of empirical research* on a topic that the researcher considers to be important. When using this tactic, one argues that, although little research has been conducted on a particular area, a greater understanding of this topic or area is essential to progress in the field. This strategy can be especially effective when combined with the previous tactic of presenting facts or statistics about the magnitude of the problem or issue. For example, in an article on family functioning in rural, single-parent, African American families published in *Developmental Psychology*, Brody and Flor (1997) combined tactics by opening with a statistic about their topic, and then, in a subsequent paragraph, pointing to a lack of research on this important topic:

Although migration from rural to urban areas and from the South to the North has concentrated large proportions of the African American population in Northern cities, 1 million of these families still live in the rural South (Orthner, 1986). . . . To date, very little attention has been given to understanding the ways in which rural poverty affects personal well-being, family functioning, and youth outcomes among African Americans. Most research on African American families has focused on families living in densely populated urban inner cities. Such a focus does not acknowledge the diversity of African American families and children and the variety of ways in which they respond to poverty and economic stress. (p. 1000)

Some researchers choose to begin their introduction by briefly tracing the *history of the research* on a particular area. This approach is useful when the study presents a new twist or development on a topic that has had a long history of research. Belsky (1996), for example, took this approach in an article published in *Developmental Psychology* about father-infant attachment. He began his article: "In the 1970s, when developmentalists initiated observational studies of the role of the father in infancy, one of the first issues addressed concerned the development of infant-father attachments" (p. 905). This opening sentence begins to set the historical context for his study – a research history that is detailed throughout the remainder of the introduction.

In addition to capturing the reader's attention, the opening segment must place the research topic in a broader context. It should provide an umbrella that will cast the project into a larger psychological or social domain. By setting a context, the author focuses the reader within a particular framework, complete with that domain's traditions, terms, and methodology. The more concisely one can frame the general domain of the study, the more likely the subsequent literature review will be focused and concise.

The techniques described above can attract the reader's attention and place the study in a broader context; however, they are by no means exhaustive. Although creative writing is not always appropriate in subsequent sections of a research article, creativity in the introductory segment can give an article a unique appeal.

SECTION II: THE LITERATURE REVIEW

The main feature of the second segment of the introduction is an illustrative, although not exhaustive, review of the extant literature surrounding the topic of study. It is customary that the important and relevant works in the area of research be cited. The author can assume that the reader is informed about the general principles of the domain and should keep the review succinct. Later in the paper, such as in the discussion section, the findings of the present research report will be integrated with the other studies. The author should include in the literature review all of the studies that will be discussed later, because it is not recommended that new articles be introduced in the discussion section.

The literature review should be presented in a coherent, integrated fashion that links findings together around some central argument. Previous research reports can help to clarify terms, demonstrate progress in the area, or point out limitations of past research. For a longer literature review, one might consider using headings to delineate sections in which different theories, methodologies, or research traditions will be discussed. Preferences as to whether headings should be used within the introduction section vary by journal editors, so you may wish to consult the journal to which you will be submitting your article before making such a decision.

When describing the relevant studies, be sure to address the features of these studies that pertain to your manuscript. Recognize the aspects of your study that make it an improvement or advancement over past research, and review the literature with these features in mind. For example, if gender had been ignored in previous research and your study examined the role of gender, then the literature that is reviewed should state when male and when female participants were studied. Recognize the limits of the published literature and use the introduction to identify these weaknesses – after all, you will be addressing and remedying them in your research report. Consider the theoretical ramifications of the studies and be sure to introduce the theory(ies) that will be used when making sense of your findings in the discussion section.

Which studies and how much detail should be included in the literature review? It is essential to recognize the priority of the work of others and to credit relevant earlier works, but there is no need to cite tangential or overly general sources. Readers can be referred to other works as needed, but the text of your introduction should stay on a straight path set for introducing your research. It may be tempting to demonstrate just how much you know about your topic by squeezing in as many citations as you can – after all, you have probably read a great deal to become an expert on the topic of your study. However; a concise and relevant literature review will be more impressive and will convey a higher level of expertise than a lengthy and indiscriminate summary of studies. It is also important that the author be familiar with *all* of the works cited in the introduction. One surefire cue of the naiveté of an author (to a reviewer) is a misstatement or inaccurate citation of a classic in the field. Cite the accepted research and the established authorities, but do so accurately and only when appropriate to the research.

Typically, a researcher will cite many references in the literature review, although there is no magic number for deciding how many references to include. The number of citations found in literature reviews varies widely based on the scope of the topic and the quantity and quality of previous research. Regardless of the number of articles cited, neither journal editors nor readers will want to read the exhaustive details about each study mentioned. Instead, the writer should discuss only the most relevant details of the studies. The amount of detail in which to describe a previous study is determined by the purpose and nature of the present study. Whereas many reviews will discuss only main findings of studies, it may be relevant and important in setting the stage for your study to discuss other aspects of previous research, such as methodologies, participant characteristics, or the reliability and validity of measures. Use your judgment to present enough information to facilitate a sufficient understanding of your topic for an intelligent reader (although not necessarily a reader in your specific field) *without* overloading or boring the reader with extraneous information. This balance may be difficult to achieve, but it is essential in maintaining the audience's interest and understanding.

The manner in which studies are to be cited is another question often posed by novice writers. The *Publication Manual of the American Psychological Association* (APA, 1994) describes two ways of citing research: (a) Cite the authors within the sentence itself, for example, "Smith and Smith (1998) found . . .," or (b) cite the authors in parentheses at the end of a sentence, for example, "It was found that . . . (Smith & Smith, 1998)" (consult the APA *Publication Manual* for further details on citation formats). The first method – within-text citations – should primarily be reserved for studies that one plans to describe in specific detail or studies that are especially pivotal to one's argument. When one simply presents a brief summary of findings, it is preferable to avoid "name clutter" in the text by citing authors in parentheses. This method of citation is less distracting to readers, helps to avoid "laundry lists" of names, and allows the writer to integrate and condense the literature review by citing several related findings in the same sentence (see Citing Studies).

Consider these sentences from literature reviews that combine findings from several studies in a concise and integrated manner. Goldfried, Castonguay, Hayes, Drozd, and Shapiro (1997), for example, cite many diverse studies in this single sentence: "That cognitive bias and selective inattention play a significant role in perpetuating psychological disorders is a conclusion that has been drawn by therapists of different orientations (e.g., Beck, Rush, Shaw, & Emery, 1979; Klerman, Weissman, Rounsaville, & Chevron, 1984; Strupp & Binder, 1984; Wexler & Rice, 1974)" (p. 740). In the following quotation, Segrin and Abramson (1994) demonstrate how several different parentheses can be used within a sentence if one wishes to cite studies with different findings in a single sentence: "Depressed people often exhibit poor social adjustment (Gotlib & Lee, 1989), marital and family distress (Gotlib & Whiffen, 1989; Hops et al., 1987; Kahn, Coyne, & Margolin, 1985), and are rejected by their interpersonal partners (Coyne, 1976a)" (p. 655). When one considers how much more writing would have been required to convey the same findings by individually citing each study within the text, the utility of the second citation method is evident.

CITING STUDIES

- *Avoid Laundry Lists:* A literature review should not take the appearance of a "Who's Who" entry in psychology. The author should be careful to cite only the relevant studies that provide support for the point being made. Likewise, the informed literature review will be sure to mention all the critical studies from that area of research. Journal editors will notice if significant studies are omitted.

- *Avoid Stacking Abstracts:* The writer should focus on integrating the studies that make the point and avoid summarizing each finding. Stringing together summaries of studies (stacking abstracts) is the hallmark of lazy writing. The author is responsible for familiarizing himself or herself with the literature and integrating the findings for the reader.

One last point about the literature review: Avoid using direct quotes from articles reviewed unless using the author's exact words makes a *significant* contribution to the clarity or quality of your paper. Your task in writing the literature review is to read critically, synthesize, and integrate a large body of literature, and then to simplify and describe this literature for your audience *in your own words*.

SECTION III: TRANSITION TO YOUR STUDY

The third segment of an introduction provides a transition from previous research to the present study and specifically states the purpose and rationale for the present study. This section is often reserved for the closing paragraph, although it can be more than a single paragraph long. The earlier paragraphs of the introduction have set the broader stage for the paper so that the reader will not be at all surprised to learn, in this brief segment, the exact purpose(s) of the present study. Just as the opening segment and the literature review lead naturally into a description of the present study, this description will naturally lead into the next section of the paper – the methods section. This brief segment of the paper is an important transition – it is the link between what has been done in the past and what you will be describing in the rest of your paper.

There are three major aspects of a study that should be briefly covered in the transition segment of an introduction: (a) the potential implications of the study; (b) the general nature of the study; and (c) the researcher's hypotheses. This final segment of the introduction often begins by stating what the study will contribute to the existing research. This statement is invaluable – it is essentially your answer to the question, "Why have I spent my time conducting this study?" (a question implicit in the minds of reviewers, editors, and readers alike). You have just finished reviewing previous research; now state how the present study will add to, clarify, disprove, or otherwise advance what previous studies have reported. Demonstrate to your readers that your experiment is the next logical step in the research on your topic. Your literature review will have pointed out the flaws, issues, or theories that you are proposing to address or remedy, so this statement should flow naturally from a thoughtfully written review.

Once you have stated the question or problem your study will address, *briefly* lay out your plan for answering this question. This statement takes the form of a very concise summary of the nature of your experiment – more detailed information about the methods will be found in later sections. Among the information provided should be a short description of the independent and dependent variables and how they were operationalized in your study.

After laying out the research question and describing how you attempted to answer it, state your hypothesis for the outcome of the study. Hypotheses are always phrased in the past tense (e.g. "It was hypothesized," "We expected," or "The authors predicted") because the study will have already been performed. A study may have only one or several hypotheses, depending on its scope. When there are multiple hypotheses, many authors choose to demarcate them with letters or numbers at the end of this final section of the introduction.

A final segment that covers all three points will provide a smooth transition to the rest of the paper and will make the rationale and hypotheses for the study clear to the reader. The following passage from the *Journal of Consulting and Clinical Psychology* (Farrell & White, 1998) demonstrates how each element of the transition segment – summary statement of the study, hypotheses, and potential value to the literature – can be met within one paragraph.

In the present study, we examined family structure and parent-adolescent relationship variables to determine the extent to which these variables moderate the relationship between peer influences and drug use in a sample of 10th-grade adolescents. On the basis of previous literature we expected that students living in single-parent female-headed households would be more susceptible to peer influences than those living in two-parent families, as would adolescents who had poorer relationships with their parents . . . Finally, unlike many previous studies, we used a sample of students within an urban school system that serves a high percentage of African American adolescents, many of whom came from low-income families. We also examined gender differences to determine the extent to which relationships among these variables may differ for girls and boys. (p. 249)

BEYOND STRUCTURE AND ORGANIZATION

The three segments – opening, literature review, transition – can be used to organize an introduction and present the study to the reader with increasing focus: from a broad umbrella to specific statements of rationale. But this structure is not all there is to a quality introduction. Other matters, such as page length, writing quality, and tone also merit consideration as one moves from a penultimate draft to a final manuscript. Writers should consult the most recent edition of the APA *Publication Manual* (currently the 4th edition) for more specific details of manuscript preparation, as journal editors will expect that all submitted manuscripts fully conform to the standards presented in this manual (e.g., page formatting, citations, headings).

Page Length

Most APA journals will want to have the introduction limited to 5 to 9 typed manuscript pages. The lengthy literature reviews that precede doctoral dissertations are typically much too long for empirically oriented journals. Extensive literature reviews might follow a different organization and might be more appropriate for a journal that publishes literature reviews (e.g., *Psychological Bulletin*). A more useful rule for research reports would be to consider that the results are the primary focus of a data-based paper, and therefore the length of other sections can be determined largely by the length of the results section. For example, if the results section is only 1 page, then a lengthy introduction would not be warranted. In contrast, 12 pages of results would merit a lengthier introduction. When considering the length of your introduction, keep in mind that the ability to be concise is considered a prime virtue by reviewers and journal editors.

Writing Quality

As in any writing endeavor, one strives for felicity of grammar and syntax, conciseness, specific rather than vague statements, and a logical flow of ideas with clear transitions. Everything you learned in grammar classes is now relevant; make sure your subjects agree with your verbs, your tenses remain consistent, and your verbs are in the active voice. You may wish to consult the APA *Publication Manual* or other texts such as Strunk and White's (1979) *Elements of Style* to refresh yourself on matters of grammar and writing style.

Although creativity is encouraged in the conceptualization and implementation of your research, overly showy writing can be a hindrance in communicating your research to the audience. Catchy phrases may appeal to a small sample of readers, but "cutesy" does not open the door to successful journal publishing. Alliteration that does not sacrifice accuracy may be advantageous, but faddish phraseology will not add scientific merit to the research. Catch the readers' attention, and write with clarity and style, but do not use the research report as a format for stand-up comedy or romantic poetry. If you are accustomed to reading or writing for popular magazines, then it may take you some time to feel comfortable with the less flowery style of writing found in scientific journals. Read through several journal articles to get a feel for the style with which the articles are written.

WRITING STYLE

- *Concise:* Writing should be precise and unambiguous. Writers should define their terms and be clear about what they mean by them.
- *Logically Flowing:* One idea should follow from the preceding thought. The reader should be able to jump ahead and anticipate what the author is about to say.
- *Arguments should be balanced:* When establishing an argument, both sides need to be presented, so that the reader is informed about the alternative possibilities and interpretations of data. Although the author wants to present a convincing argument to establish the purpose of the study, he or she does not want to appear biased.
- *Tone:* Whenever critiquing other studies, the tone must remain professional. Criticisms should focus on theoretical and/or methodological weaknesses of the study, and not on the personal characteristics of the author.

Tone

It is essential to maintain a professional tone throughout the introduction. Although you may be criticizing previous research, differences of opinion and controversies within the field are treated with respect. When referring to a previously published study with which you disagree, it would not be apt to state that "The brevity of the report was surpassed only by the fact that it had little of substance to offer the field." Similarly, *ad hominem* statements and personal statements are of no value. Criticisms of the literature may be targeted at theoretical and/or methodological weaknesses of the cited studies, not at the personal characteristics, beliefs, or failings of the authors. There is simply no place for statements such as "Any fool would know that such findings are impossible." The following quote from an article in *Journal of Consulting and Clinical Psychology* about attrition in child therapy provides a good example of pointing out the limitations of previous research without sounding disrespectful or criticizing previous researchers themselves (Kazdin, Holland, & Crowley, 1997):

Unfortunately, the profile of characteristics that predict dropping out is not well established in large part because of salient limitations of current research. First, the range of variables examined in research has been limited in number and scope. Typically, "variables of convenience" (e.g. socioeconomic disadvantage, marital status) are selected as predictors because they can be retrieved from clinic intake forms. Second, the predictors usually encompass broad characteristics that neither shed light on the possible mechanisms involved in dropping out nor suggest guidelines for where, when, and how to intervene to prevent dropping out. . . . Third and related, research has not been driven by conceptual models regarding what variables might be involved or how they interface with participation in treatment. (p. 453).

Another point to keep in mind when critiquing previous research is that one should strive to construct a balanced argument. Recognize the strengths along with the weaknesses of the studies under review. An argument will receive more credibility if the author appears reasonable and open-minded rather than overly biased and critical.

Maintaining a professional tone also requires that one not exaggerate the importance of his or her own study. Recognize that your study has a limited scope and write accordingly. Never state that your study will "prove" or "solve" anything, or even provide irrefutable results. The introduction establishes the importance of the study, but reviewers and readers will be quick to notice when this importance has been blown out of proportion.

Revise, Revise, and Revise Again

Once you have written a draft, read and revise it with an eye toward reducing excessive wordiness, clarifying confusing or vague statements, and identifying words that have multiple meanings. Keep in mind that the meaning you intended to convey may not always be communicated to the reader. For instance, imagine that your introduction reviewed studies that compared cognitive-behavioral therapy to medication for the treatment of anxiety disorders. You report that the cognitive-behavioral group had less relapse following treatment. This may appear clear to you; however, the word "group" has two possible meanings. It may suggest to a reader that the treatment was provided in a group format, whereas in actuality you were referring to the group (the treatment condition) of clients treated individually. Unclear statements such as this may be easy for the author to miss, but they can make the research report very difficult for the reader to understand.

Read the draft more than once, have a set of outsider eyes provide comments, and sleep on and reread the manuscript one more time before submission. Be your own critic. Of course, the facetious and fussy reviewers and action editor will always be able to find recommended changes that you missed. Steel yourself to this feedback; it doesn't hurt physically and it will help your paper to communicate to other readers.

CONCLUSION

Writing an introduction requires flexibility within a framework. Certain components are typically present (the opening paragraph, the literature review, the transitional), but the actual composition of each section varies from article to article. To use an analogy germane to current psychotherapy research, the use of manuals in psychological treatment has been criticized for being rigid and stifling creativity.

However, for manuals to be effective they must be applied flexibly. The components of any given manual are standardized (e.g., building a relationship, identification of self talk, homework), but the specific content (e.g., test anxiety, loss of parent, interpersonal dejection) and the application of the exact techniques (e.g., playing a game, using a workbook) may vary to meet the individualized needs of the client. Likewise, the sections of an introduction can take on many different "looks" depending on the purpose of the study. The literature review may explain a broad domain of psychology or focus on a detailed subset of research. The tone of the writing may be supportive or critical of past research. The hypotheses can be exploratory or predetermined. The key is communicating ideas with clarity and accuracy. How this is accomplished remains the prerogative of the author.

REFERENCES

American Psychological Association. (1994). *Publication manual of the American Psychological Association* (4th ed.). Washington, DC: Author.

Beck, A. T., Rush, A. J., Shaw, B. F., & Emery, G. (1979). *Cognitive therapy of depression*. New York: Guilford Press.

Belsky, J. (1996). Parent, infant, and social-contextual antecedents of father-son attachment security. *Developmental Psychology, 32,* 905–913.

Brody, G. H., & Flor, D. L. (1997). Maternal psychological functioning, family processes, and child adjustment in rural, single-parent, African American families. *Developmental Psychology, 33,* 1000–1011.

Coyne, J. C. (1976). Depression and the response of others. *Journal of Abnormal Psychology, 85,* 186–193.

Farrell, A. D. & White, K. S. (1998). Peer influences and drug use among urban adolescents: Family structure and parent-adolescent relationship as protective factors. *Journal of Consulting and Clinical Psychology, 66,* 248–258.

Goldfried, M. R., Castonguay, L. G., Hayes, A. M., Drozd, J. F., & Shapiro, D. A. (1997). A comparative analysis of the therapeutic focus in cognitive-behavioral and psychodynamic-interpersonal sessions. *Journal of Consulting & Clinical Psychology, 65,* 740–748.

Gotlib, I. H., & Lee, C. M. (1989). The social functioning of depressed patients: A longitudinal assessment. *Journal of Social & Clinical Psychology, 8,* 223–237.

Gotlib, I. H., & Whiffen, V. E. (1989). Depression and marital functioning: An examination of specificity and gender differences. *Journal of Abnormal Psychology, 98,* 23–30.

Hops, H., Biglan, A., Sherman, L., Arthur, J., Friedman, L., & Osteen, V. (1987). Home observations of family interactions of depressed women. *Journal of Consulting & Clinical Psychology, 55,* 341–346.

Kahn, J., Coyne, J. C., & Margolin, G. (1985). Depression and marital disagreement: The social construction of despair. *Journal of Social and Personal Relationships, 2,* 447–461.

Kazdin, A. E., Holland, L., & Crowley, M. (1997). Family experience of barriers to treatment and premature termination from child therapy. *Journal of Consulting & Clinical Psychology, 65,* 453–463.

Kendall, P. C., Finch, A. J., & Montgomery, L. E. (1978). Vicarious anxiety: A systematic evaluation of a vicarious threat to self-esteem. *Journal of Consulting & Clinical Psychology, 46,* 997–1008.

Klerman, G. L., Weissman, M. M., Rounsaville, B., & Chevron, E. (1984). *Interpersonal psychotherapy of depression.* New York: Basic Books.

Maguire, K., & Pastore, A. L. (1995). *Bureau of Justice Statistics: Sourcebook of Criminal Justice Statistics—1994.* Washington, DC: U.S. Department of Justice.

Megargee, E. I. (1997). Using the Megargee MMPI-based classification system with the MMPI-2s of female prison inmates. *Psychological Assessment, 9,* 75–82.

Orthner, D. (1986). *Children and families in the South: Trends in health care, family services, and the rural economy* (Prepared statement for a hearing before the U.S. House of Representatives Select Committee on Children, Youth, and Families, Macon, GA). Washington, DC: U.S. Government Printing Office.

Segrin, C., & Abramson, L. Y. (1994). Negative reactions to depressive behaviors: A communication theories analysis. *Journal of Abnormal Psychology, 103,* 655–668.

Strunk, W., Jr., & White, E. B. (1979). *The elements of style* (3rd ed.). New York: Macmillan.

Strupp, H. H., & Binder, J. (1984). *Psychotherapy in a new key.* New York: Basic Books.

Wexler, D. A., & Rice, L. N. (1974). *Innovations in client-centered psychotherapy.* New York: Wiley.

Wilson, T. D., Houston, C. E., Etling, K. M., & Brekke, N. (1996). A new look at anchoring effects: Basic anchoring and its antecedents. *Journal of Experimental Psychology: General, 125,* 387–402.

Chapter 5

Theories and Hypotheses

ABRAHAM TESSER

An essay with this title could be written by almost any working social scientist but the form, shape, and content would differ considerably among authors. As a past journal editor and chair of a grants review committee, I have had many opportunities to compose and to systematically read reviews of research. One thing that almost all critics agree on is the importance of theory. Research training for most of us is very clear on how to use statistics to evaluate data; many of us have been exposed to a substantial dose of material on experimental design (e.g., the circumstances under which it is or is not possible to draw causal inferences). Still, in spite of its importance, few of us have had much formal training in "theory." We pick up much of what we know from our own resonances to the literature in combination with the informal comments of instructors and fellow graduate students and, later, colleagues. There is little in the way of a theory "canon" that all of us study. So, although there is widespread agreement on the importance of theory and hypotheses to research each of us tends to emphasize different aspects in thinking about it. Thus, the issues and the emphases in this treatment are admittedly idiosyncratic.

I think of theories as abstract schemes that help to explain and organize experience. For present purposes, hypotheses are derivations from a more general theory and are often tied to concrete obser-

The author gratefully acknowledges the helpful comments of Ileana Arias, Mike Kernis, and Rich Marsh and the support of NIMH grant K05 MH01233.

vations. The line between what is an hypothesis and what is a theory is often fuzzy. I will often use the word *idea* to refer to either.

This chapter focuses on the factors associated with the impact of an idea. Rather than review formal treatments of theory construction, I present examples of personally interesting theories and hypotheses. This is followed by some notes on how to avoid boring ideas and then some informal principles for constructing interesting ideas. Rather than focus on the formal evaluation of theories and hypotheses, I provide some thoughts on the psychology of what makes a theory or hypothesis credible.

HIGH-IMPACT THEORIES AND HYPOTHESES (OR WILL MY IDEA BE CITED?)

Philosophers of science provide us with a number of useful dimensions for evaluating theory, such as parsimony, variety of observations accounted for, and so on (e.g., Jones, 1985). Although these attributes are important in a formal evaluation of a theory, I would like to focus on something more informal but perhaps at least as important: the *impact* of the theory or hypothesis. By impact I mean the extent to which people *use* the theory in explaining relevant phenomena. Although a theoretical idea is usually broader than what is captured by a single study, the modal number of citations for a single journal article is zero[1]. The formal adequacy of a theory is irrelevant if the theory is not used either as a way of understanding the world, explaining data (that fit or do not fit the theory), or as a standard against which to evaluate another theory. I speculate that at least four factors play a prominent role in determining the impact of an idea: the style with which it is written, the zeitgeist of the field, the interest value of the idea, and the credibility of the idea.

---

[1] Simonton (1985) studied the careers of 10 distinguished psychologists, G. Allport, A. Bandura, D. T. Campbell, J.P. Guilford, C. I. Hovland, W. Kohler, C. R. Rogers, B. F. Skinner, K. W. Spence, and E. C. Tolman. Simonton distinguished major articles from minor articles. Forty-four percent of the senior authored articles of these giants were minor articles, that is, had not a single citation over a 5-year period!

Writing

Because an idea must be communicated to have impact, it is difficult to put too much stress on the importance of writing quality. Therefore, I feel compelled to plug Chapter 11 of this volume, which focuses on writing, and make a few, very brief comments. Ideas that are written well enough to be accompanied by the click of "I get it!" or well enough to show their broad applicability are more likely to be used and cited. Work through a good style manual (e.g., Strunk & White, 1959) and have colleagues read and comment on preliminary drafts of your article. In evaluating solicited comments or more formal comments from reviewers try not to be defensive: Assume that the commentators are smart and trying to be helpful. It is not their fault if they don't understand what you thought was clear. Enough said, here.

An Aside on Citations

According to the conventional wisdom, there is nothing sweeter than the sound of one's name. The corollary is that there is nothing sweeter than to see one's own name cited. One's own name is very easily noticed (Moray, 1959) and will attract attention. Such increased attention and additional processing will make the work more memorable to the people who are cited. Greater memorability of your work will pay off in the coin of the realm, greater likelihood of your work being cited, at least by those whose name you have mentioned. On the other hand, a text strewn with citations is more difficult and tedious to read. So, there is a danger of losing consumers whose names haven't been mentioned. Clearly, only work that is relevant should be cited. However, the threshold for relevance is not fixed and the number of citations is to some extent a stylistic matter (see Chapter 10).

Zeitgeist

By zeitgeist I refer to the broad point of view taken by a field at some particular point in time. The zeitgist in psychology changed when a predominantly behaviorist approach gave way to an openly cognitive approach. Now, given the current national interest, the scientific breakthroughs, and the research support for neuroscience, I believe that psychology is on the cusp of a revolution in which many of the subfields will be informed by neuropsychological mechanisms and computer simulations of such mechanisms. Subdisciplines too are subject to periods when a particular phenomenon or approach is hot. As I was entering social psychology, group dynamics had its heyday and cognitive-consistency theories were important. Then there was wide interest in attribution theory and phenomena; and now there is strong interest in in-group/out-group phenomena, automatic versus controlled processes, and attachment phenomena.

Ideas that are consistent with the current zeitgist are more likely to have impact, at least in the short run, than ideas that are not. Zeitgeist ideas are simply likely to be relevant to more researchers. Such ideas will inform the work of many in an easy to understand way due to shared assumptions and a shared research base. Because zeitgist-related ideas are more likely to inform the work of others they are more likely to be cited. Finally, zeitgist-related work may be impactful because it is more likely to cite people who are currently publishing, thereby making the work more memorable to them. If it is more memorable, it is more likely to be cited.

The suggestion that the impact of a theory or hypothesis may be at least partially independent of its formal quality is not a new idea. However, the prominence of the suggestion to simply follow the zeitgist to give your ideas impact sounds crass, even to me. The truth is that by the time a point of view becomes mainstream, I find it less interesting (see below) and tend not to read it (unless, of course, I see my own name). Perhaps a more important determinant of the impact of an hypothesis or theoretical idea is its interest value.

INTERESTING THEORIES AND HYPOTHESES: S-IDEAS AND B-IDEAS[2]

For many, myself included, it is the beauty of ideas that keeps us in psychology; seeing the world in certain ways provokes a positive, almost sensual experience. These are the kind of ideas that have impact. What are the characteristics of such ideas? Certainly, ideas that are described by language that is usually reserved for sex or the

---

[2] This section is based on an unpublished talk (Tesser, 1990).

kind of hot pastrami sandwich one can get only in New York City are special. I call ideas that are powerful enough to provoke positive sensual responses S-ideas[3]. Below I describe some types of S-ideas. (Although the examples come from social psychology the principles should be applicable to any area of psychology.) Then I mention two factors underlying boring or B-ideas. Some thoughts on how to develop S-ideas and avoid B-ideas are also included.

Types of S-Ideas

Common Cause. The world is a chaotic, buzzing, confusing place full of things and events that appear to be totally unrelated to one another. Ideas that show how seemingly disparate, dissimilar events can be the result of the same process are a type of S-idea. To Solomon Asch's (1956) surprise, when faced with the unanimous judgments of others, even when those judgments were obviously and blatantly wrong, individuals conformed on about one-third of the trials. What does this finding have to do with the following incident? As Andrew Mormille rode home to Manhattan on the A train, he was stabbed to death in plain sight of 11 witnesses who did nothing about it, not even calling the police, even though his attackers had left the car (Darley & Latané, 1968).

It took the genius of Bibb Latané and John Darley (1970) to show us that Asch's observations are fundamental to understanding such incidents. Bystanders are usually not callous and indifferent to the victim's plight. According to Darley and Latané's S-idea, the failure to intervene is often the playing out of powerful interpretational and conformity forces in ambiguous situations. Insights like this, which allow us to see two apparently very different-looking situations as being the result of the same processes, are S-ideas.

Surprising Implications of the Banal. Some S-ideas are unsurprising, obvious, and even banal in themselves. Their "S-ence" comes

---

[3] The "S" designation in this context is appropriate for a couple of reasons. Not only is it intended to bring to mind sensual images but one can also image the chewing on and ingesting of a delicious idea. The Yiddish word for eat is *ess* [transliteration]. Aron and Aron (1986) have devoted an entire book to the appreciation of such ideas in social psychology. Other theorists talk about similar experiences in a variety of domains under the label *flow* (Csikszentmihalyi, 1982) or *dynamic orientation* (Wicklund, 1986).

from their rather surprising implications. For example, the notion that people tend to be consistent is so obviously true that even one's grandmother takes it for granted. But, when pushed by people like Leon Festinger (1957), the idea that people are consistent leads to the rather surprising and well-replicated prediction that the *less* the reward or the greater the punishment for engaging in a particular activity, the *more* positive the evaluation of the activity.

An even more banal observation is that people like to see and present themselves as skilled, capable, competent performers. This rather obvious idea has been converted by many people into S-ideas. One of my favorite conversions is that by Stephen Berglas and Ned Jones (1978). Their work on self-handicapping showed that the desire to look good is so strong that people will actually handicap themselves (e.g., take debilitating drugs) so that if they don't succeed they can blame the drug.

The Power of the Bizarre. Some S-ideas are just plain bizarre. They appear to be obviously wrong. However, if you suspend your skepticism and take them seriously, they provide a powerful way of organizing and predicting experience. Einstein's idea that the speed of light was *not* relative to the speed of the observer was such an idea. Bem's (1965) self-perception theory is also such an idea. To put it simply, the theory asserts that people really don't know themselves in any "special" way. Often they have no easily accessible internal attitude or feeling. So, when asked, people respond with an inference based on observation of their public behavior and the circumstances surrounding it. This is exactly the way in which we know *other* people. These days, we take self-perception notions to be obvious. They are quite consistent with the zeitgist in cognitive social psychology. At the time it was introduced, it seemed like a crazy idea. It was inconsistent with self-insight approaches to counseling (e.g., Rogers, 1961); it was inconsistent with common sense. In short, it had the appearance of being obviously wrong. Even today it jars, at least it does so for me. It implies that much of what I know about my own "private" likes and dislikes comes from public sources.

Bem's bizarre idea is an S-idea. By assuming that it is true, we can understand a lot of behavior. We can understand ordinary, everyday events; for example, why people like brown bread (because they see themselves eating it). It gives us an alternative explanation for some of the surprising consistency-theory results alluded to above. For example, people who are paid only $1 for telling a lie come to believe that lie more than people who are paid $20 to tell the lie (Festinger & Carlsmith, 1959). (Bem's [1967] explanation: If it took $20 to get me to say X is true, I probably don't believe X; if it took only $1 to get me to say X is true, I probably believed X to begin with.) It also helps explain why persons who are induced to do a small favor can later, more easily, be induced to do a large favor (Cialdini, 1985). (If I do a small favor I see myself as the kind of person who is helpful.) Finally, this bizarre idea can even explain a well-replicated phenomenon that defies common sense. Deci (1971) and his colleagues, for example, have found that if you reward people for doing what they like to do, they sometimes lose their intrinsic interest in doing it. Why should reward reduce interest in something that people like to do? Again, Bem's S-idea comes to the rescue (Lepper, Greene, & Nisbett, 1978). If I infer my self-interest from my behavior, then seeing myself doing X for some external reward implies that I must not like X. Therefore, subsequently, I no longer choose it.

Order in Chaos. Sometimes S-ideas grow out of disorder, incon-sistency, and contradiction. One of the earliest topics in social psy-chology concerned the effects of coactors on the performance of actors (Allport, 1920; Triplett, 1898). However, in spite of its obvious centrality and relevance to the field, the topic was dropped. Why? I think it was because it was frustrating to work on. Sometimes the presence of coacting organisms would facilitate performance (e.g., Travis, 1925) and, unpredictably, in other cases it would undermine performance (e.g., Pessin, 1933). The area was a mess until 1965.

Zajonc (1965) brought order to this chaos by suggesting that the presence of conspecifics raises arousal. Prior research (e.g., Spence, Farber, & McFann, 1956) had shown that arousal increases the likeli-hood of dominant responses and, therefore, facilitates performance on simple tasks (where correct responses are dominant) and under-mines performance on complex tasks (where incorrect response[s] are dominant). With this idea, one could go back and classify the tasks in prior studies as to whether they were simple or complex. Sure enough, the presence of coactors (or an audience) facilitated performance on simple tasks such as winding fishing reels but interfered with performance on complex tasks such as learning nonsense syllables. This S-idea brought order to what had been chaos and revitalized the area of research.

Formal Statements. Mathematical models also can be S-ideas. The S-ence of formal models lies in their parsimony. Mathematical formulations pack a host of insights into a deceptively short, succinct statement. I believe some of the "new" mathematics (e.g., Gleick, 1987), for example, nonlinear dynamics, packs a lot of excitement and, at this time, promise for psychology. These formulations capture aspects of behavior that intuitively we know is present but that tend not to be represented in most of our present thinking. For example, sometimes very small changes in a situation can lead to large, abrupt shifts in behavior; sometimes conflicting forces do not result in averaging but rather they result in bimodality, with some people going in one direction and others in the opposite direction.

These intuitions, and others, are captured in computer simulations with nonlinear processing rules in which the final state of the system is an iterative function of the starting state of the system. A nice example of this is Nowak, Szamrej, and Latané's (1990) work on the distribution of attitudes in a population. Starting with a random spatial distribution of attitudes in favor of or against "X," and assuming that influence is a function of proximity and number of agreeing and disagreeing others, their simulations show the following with astonishing regularity: The random distribution of attitudes changes so that there are spatial "clumps" of like-minded people; that the majority opinion tends to increase in frequency and the minority to decrease, but that the minority opinion does not disappear regardless of the length of the simulation.

Abelson (1995) has summarized several factors underlying theoretical interest in an argument. His suggestions are broad and do a nice job of accounting for the examples I have just described. He suggests that an argument "is scientifically interesting when it has the potential to change what scientists believe about important causal relationships" (p. 158). Also important to theoretical interest are the surprisingness of the account (but the claim cannot be too incredible to be true) and the importance of the account, that is, the number of pertinent relationships for which it has implications.

S-ideas are wonderful. They should and they do have impact. Clearly the examples I chose are not a definitive list. They are merely my own, idiosyncratic choices. S-ideas are contrasted with B- (boring) ideas. Again, it is important to emphasize the personal nature of these judgments. One person's B-idea might very well be another's S-idea and vice versa. Manuscripts concerning B-ideas are often returned to authors with the advice that they "sharpen the theoretical aspects of their work."

B-Ideas: What They Are and How to Avoid Them

I call boring ideas B-ideas. My informal observations suggest that there are at least two principles that seem to underlie many B-ideas. Below I sketch out those principles: how they work and how to avoid them.

Balance Principle. One of the most powerful ideas in social psychology is Heider's (1958) Balance Principle: the notion that good things are seen to go with good things and bad things to go with bad things. Unfortunately, this principle is so strong that often it is all that sustains some hypotheses in the social sciences. That is, some hypotheses simply reflect the playing out of this principle rather than observation of the real world or some logical reasoning process. Balanced hypotheses have a ring of plausibility but with closer scrutiny often turn out to be hollow.

The principle is easiest to see in theorizing involving individual differences (although it is clearly present in experimental work as well). The general form is "good guys" do good things, "bad guys" do bad things. The original work on locus of control (Rotter, 1966) is certainly not B research but this dimension can be made to fit this kind of thinking. Having an internal locus of control was often seen as "better" than having an external locus of control, that is, internals are the good guys, externals are the bad guys. Here are some balanced hypotheses from different areas. From education: Internals are more likely to profit from a new instructional method than externals. From business: Internals use more innovative marketing strategies than externals. The interesting thing about each of these B formulations is that they can be causally reversed and remain equally appealing. For example, exposure to this new instructional method is likely to result in a more internal orientation.[4] I am not arguing that "balanced" formulations are necessarily wrong. My objection is simply that balanced thinking is not necessarily useful.

There are ways to combat the balance principle. For example, one can change the name of the independent or the dependent variable to a name that captures the meaning of the variable but does so with neutral or opposite-valenced words. One might think of internals as bullheaded or people who blame themselves for things that go wrong. Now, substitute the new label into the formulation and see if it still works. For example, instead of "Internals are more likely to profit from the new instructional program," suppose we say "Self-blamers are more likely to profit from the program." If the formulation still works, perhaps there is something to it. If not, the formulation may be no more than the playing out of the balance principle.

Another way of combating the balance principle is to assume that its opposite is true and then try to explain it. For example, let's assume that externals profit more than internals from the innovative new educational program. How is that possible? Perhaps the material being learned was not of personal interest and the internals may not have paid as much attention to it as did externals. Or perhaps the program is embedded in an educational context that provides little choice and the internals are turned off by that context. From these explanations comes a richer, more interesting theoretical understanding. Rather than internals being more likely to profit from this new program, we have the following: When the material is personally engaging, internals are more likely to profit from the new program; or, When the new program is embedded in a context of free choice, internals are more likely to benefit than externals. In short, the balance principle can be finessed if recognized and explicitly dealt with.

Total Reliance on Intuition. The second principle underlying many B-formulations is the *total* reliance on intuition. This comes in two forms that are indistinguishable in their content, but quite different in process. Reliance on someone else's intuition is the lower form.

---

[4] It is easiest to make this point using examples of application because there is usually consensus on what the "good" behavior is. However, this type of thinking is evident in basic research as well.

I call it the Marty Principle. It gets its name from the play, *Marty*, by Paddy Chayefsky. Marty is a single, middle-aged butcher who spends his free time "hanging out" with his friends. One of the most memorable parts of dialogue goes like this: "What do you feel like doing tonight?" "I don't know. What do you feel like doing tonight?" And so it goes, repeated over and over and over, from dyad to dyad, and back again. I know colleagues who theorize precisely this way. They generate a potential design and ask their students or colleagues, "What do you think will happen in this cell? Or, that cell?" This kind of theorizing often produces the same stultifying, directionless, and defeating products as does the dialogue in Chayefsky's play. The second form of this principle is total reliance on one's own intuition. Although this form represents a step up (one person's intuition is likely to be more coherent), it is not a cure. In my view, in general, *total* reliance on intuition is a mistake

Intuition is often wrong. Sometimes we rely on the intuitions of our research participants. There is now a large literature detailing the problems with role-play studies in which participants are asked to "intuit" how they would behave, given a particular set of circumstances (e.g., Aronson, Wilson, & Brewer, 1998). But even professional, well-trained and well-paid intuitionists can be wrong. You may recall that Stanley Milgram (1974) asked 40 psychiatrists how they thought his experiment on obedience would turn out. They were totally wrong. If Milgram relied on these intuitions, the study never would have been done. Not only is intuition often wrong, it is often commonplace and uninteresting. If investigators relied totally on intuition, many of the surprising studies that we love telling our classes about would never have been run.

Does that mean that intuition is always bad? No. Does it mean we should never discuss an idea with others? Again, no. Intuition and discussion with others have their place. Indeed, intuition is a great place to start developing principles of behavior. Once the principle is developed, however, put your intuition away. The dissonance principle – inconsistency is aversive – is a nice intuitive principle. Once one has arrived at that principle, however, intuition is no longer necessary. It should not be allowed to interfere with the design of experiments intended to test the principle or the derivations of its implications. In designing the study, don't develop an intuitive account of each cell taken individually. If necessary, to keep your intuition at bay, translate your operations into theoretical language. For example, don't think of a dollar as money but rather as one unit of justification and $20 as 20 units of justification. When deriving hypotheses from your intuitively arrived at principle, the criterion for the derivation should move toward formal logic rather than intuitive plausibility. Indeed, the more implausible the derivation from a plausible principle the more interesting the work is likely to be.

Commonplace intuitions can be converted from B-ideas to S-ideas if they are stated with audacity. One intuitively appealing proposition, for example, is that persons act toward their spouse the way they acted toward their mother. Hazan and Shaver (Hazan & Shaver, 1987) actually had the nerve to take this bit of "Bubba psychology" seriously and have created some of the most interesting research being done in interpersonal relationships today. Developmental psychologists (e.g., Ainsworth, Blehar, Waters, & Wall, 1978) have convincingly argued that the relationship between a child and a parent can be secure, anxious-ambivalent, or avoidant. Hazan and Shaver (1987) reasoned that if these kinds of attachment styles characterize adult relationships, then persons with different styles should experience love differently and should have different ideologies concerning love. Indeed, avoidant lovers fear closeness, and do not feel accepted; anxious-ambivalent lovers show emotional extremes and jealousy in relationships; secure lovers experience love in terms of happiness, friendship, and trust. Their ideologies also differ. Avoidant lovers see intense romantic love as being common at the beginning of a relationship, but rarely lasting; anxious-ambivalent persons believe that there aren't many people as willing as they are to commit themselves to long-term relationships. The mental model of the securely attached lover is that people seem to be well intentioned and have their heart in the right place.

Pretty nifty work, right? But what makes it so? It was the guts to take an intuitive insight seriously, and the willingness to work out its *logical* consequences. It is the demonstration of the logical deductions that gives the whole thing its S-ence. It is perhaps worth noting here, however, that an interesting idea, even one as exciting as that by Hazan and Shaver, can't salvage lack of originality and insight. Not long after Hazan and Shaver's work appeared, the literature seemed to explode with work intended to elaborate and extend their thesis.

Some of this work is brilliant but much of it is stultifying, relatively thoughtless exercises attempting to demonstrate that attachment style is related to any other variable that can be imagined and measured. Clearly, the B-ideas in mindless work show through even when the work is intended to elaborate a great idea.

SOURCES OF INTERESTING HYPOTHESES

To this point, I have talked about S-ideas and some causes and cures for B-ideas. My informal observations of the research process have also left me with several notions about the psychology of generating interesting hypotheses or S-ideas.[5] Let me share a few of these with you.

Inventing Reality

S-ideas are more likely to come from the assumption that the world is invented, not discovered. Certainly there are "real" experiences "out there" but they don't become interesting until they are interpreted. And there is no "true" interpretation. There only are more or less interesting ways of organizing that experience. Take for example the 1 dollar/20 dollar experiment that I described earlier. People do come to believe a lie they told for $1 more than a lie they told for $20. Why? It could be that people dislike inconsistency (Festinger & Carlsmith, 1959); it could be self-perception (Bem, 1972); it could be self-presentation (Tedeschi, Schlenker, & Bonoma, 1971); it could be a response to an ego threat (Steele, 1988). All of these hypotheses are plausible ways of explaining exactly the same phenomenon. And all of them have a database that gives them some credibility. Which is true?

They are all true (or false) under certain circumstances. And the more interesting an investigator finds an interpretation, the more likely he or she is to find or invent circumstances under which the favored interpretation is true (McGuire, 1973). One corollary of the

---

[5] Some of the ideas presented here have been discussed earlier by McGuire (1973, 1983, 1997). Weick (1989) also presents a very helpful discussion of some of the issues.

invention-of-reality principle is that "believing is seeing." Once you begin to believe a particular explanation, then illustrations of that principle pop up quite easily.

A discovery set, assuming that the world is discovered, not invented, can, but is less likely to, lead to S-ideas than an invention set, at least in social psychology. A discovery set usually results in a fact-gathering research style. The idea is that if one looks long enough and gathers enough facts, then by somehow juxtaposing those facts, nature will reveal herself. This way of doing research strikes me as an asocial variant of the Marty Principle. Rather than asking subjects and colleagues what they think, the investigator asks the data to announce their meaning. In some instances, exploratory factor analysis may exemplify this approach. The problem is that data, by themselves, are almost infinitely multifaceted. Without some imposed (invented) order, often the data cannot tell a coherent story.

Catholicism in Focus

Psychology is about what people think, feel, and do to themselves and one another in the course of living their lives. Psychology is clearly more than what currently appears in any particular psychology journal. Many of the S-ideas I described earlier were not extensions of what was currently popular in the literature. There was practically no work on prosocial behavior or altruism prior to Darley and Latané's start. The work on love is flourishing but was nowhere to be found in the journals until Hatfield and Berscheid (e.g., Berscheid & Walster [Hatfield], 1978) decided to pursue it. The list of relevant topics in psychology on which little work has been done is almost endless. For example, if I had the time, I would think about gossip and rumor (e.g., Rosnow, 1991), humor, and the determinants of choice of entertainment (e.g., Zillman & Bryant, 1985). So, if you have a particular interest but it is not a topic that is currently being pursued, jump in. If you can avoid the balance trap and *total* immersion in intuition, then a new area is more likely to produce an S-idea than one that already has been plowed.

There is a corollary to the catholicism notion. If we are to have confidence in a finding or an interpretation and if the discipline is to advance, then follow-up work is a necessary and an important function. However, if the goal is to produce an S-idea then base your research on your own *informed* observation and understanding of people, not someone else's study. (Research that is *uninformed* by related theoretical and empirical work is more likely to reinvent the wheel than to produce some interesting new breakthrough.) To show that someone else's work is difficult to replicate or is based on an artifact is important to the cumulative nature of the science but in my opinion will not produce a particularly interesting new idea.

Moderation in Abstraction

There appears to be an optimal level of abstraction for productive research. In 1945, Prescott Lecky developed the abstract thesis that inconsistency is aversive and that therefore people seek consistency. Although there was some acknowledgment of that position in the field, the position produced less research and interest, in my opinion, than the less abstract idea that the inconsistency between attitudes and behavior is painful (dissonance theory), or that inconsistency between one's own and another's view of self is painful (e.g., Higgins, 1987; Swann, 1983). The least abstract hypotheses are not necessarily the most productive. For example, less abstract versions of these hypotheses are "Inconsistency between political attitudes and voting is uncomfortable" or "Extraverts don't like people who think they are introverts." It seems to me that the lowest level, like the highest level, of abstraction is less interesting and of lesser heuristic value than the middle level statements.

Mechanisms, Mechanisms, Mechanisms

People like a good story. Characters and events are the ingredients of a story but without a plot they are not a story. Readers want to know why the characters did what they did and how the events are linked. Scientists are, in some ways, like people. They like a good theory. Variables and relationships are the ingredients of a theory but without a mechanism they are not a theory. A focus on mechanism is more likely to produce an S-idea than a focus on more variables or correlations. (If thinking mechanism, mechanism, mechanism makes the research process sound too mechanical, then think process, process, process, or plot, plot, plot.)

Science as a Dialectic: Thesis, Antithesis, Synthesis

Nature likes to keep things in bounds. When the occasion calls for it, we are aggressive, but not too aggressive; we are helpful, but not too helpful; and so on. It is almost as if the goads to our aggressiveness or helpfulness also contain within them inhibitors. For example, the vigor of another's attack induces aggression but that same vigor can also make us afraid; another's dependency can open us up but at the same time cause us to withdraw out of concern for getting drawn in too far. I find it useful in generating hypotheses to think of science as a dialectic. In discussing the balance principle I foreshadowed my strategy here. For any thesis, generate the antithesis and propose a synthesis.

This principle has proved useful in my own work. For example, a close other's outstanding performance can produce negative affect such as jealousy (e.g., Salovey & Rodin, 1984) but it can also produce positive affect, a kind of "basking in reflected glory" (Cialdini et al., 1976). The synthesis provided by the self-evaluation maintenance model (Tesser, 1988) suggests that jealousy will result when the performance dimension is high in relevance to one's self-definition and basking will result when it is low.

CREDIBLE THEORIES AND HYPOTHESES

If a theory is to have impact and be used by others it has to be known to the consumer, plausible/believable, or both. In talking about writing, the zeitgist, and interesting formulations, the focus was on the attributes of a theory or hypothesis that will increase its likelihood of being remembered. Well-known theories are not always used because consumers believe them. Often well-known ideas become targets, sometimes even straw men, to be disproved or ridiculed.

In this section we explore some of the issues concerning the credibility of theories. Again, the focus is not on formal attributes of good theories. Rather, the focus is on the informal, more psychological variables associated with credibility. We will see that the zeitgeist and some of the things said about interesting ideas play a role here as well. Indeed, one issue that makes a big difference in the receipt of an idea is whether consumers have an already formulated theory or schema for thinking about the research domain.

De Nova Research

If your thesis is about a relatively new topic or phenomenon, most consumers will not have a preformed or favorite explanation of their own, and this will affect how they react to your new hypothesis. My guess is that there will be a minority of consumers who will insist that this is not really "psychology." The newer the phenomenon and the less visible the scientist, the more likely it is that a consumer will have this dismissive reaction.

A new idea may be given little more than a cursory reading. Potential consumers may feel "This has nothing to do with what I am doing. I'm too busy to be very concerned with this." Petty and Cacciopo (1986) make a distinction between central and peripheral processing (see also Chaiken, 1987). The kind of response we are discussing here will lead to peripheral processing at best. Without strong motivation to read your idea, its credibility is not likely to depend on the cogency of your argument (a feature that is important in central processing) but rather on peripheral cues: the visibility of the scientist proposing the idea (have a well-known coauthor, perhaps), the quality of the journal in which it appears (be persistent), and perhaps even the length of the paper.

Let us suppose that your idea is published in an easily accessible form and a number of potential consumers actually read it carefully. If they have no preconceived notions of their own, what are the features of a theory that will make it credible? Thagard (1989; see also Read & Marcus-Newhall, 1993) has proposed several principles of "explanatory coherence" or goodness/acceptability of an explanation. The principles of breadth and simplicity are straightforward. Consumers prefer theories that explain more of the data to theories that explain less. Consumers prefer simpler, more parsimonious explanations, to more complicated, elaborate explanations. Consumers of explanations aren't into Hollywood solutions, for example, the hero finds, for some inexplicable reason, the money he needs to save his family. Rather, they prefer explanations that entail elements that can in turn be explained. Kelley's (1973) "discounting principle" for social perception is consistent with Thagard's principle that explanations are comparative, that is, an account will be credible to the extent that there are few or no competing accounts for the same phenomena. Finally, an explanation will be credible if the consumer can call up an analogous explanatory mechanism from another domain. For example, I find the principles alluded to here for understanding scientific theories more credible because they are quite analogous to principles of person perception with which I am familiar.

Jurors are like consumers of research. They have data, that is, the facts of the case, and they are confronted by at least two competing theories: that of the prosecution and that of the defense. Which theory will they believe? The work of Pennington and Hastie (1992) resonates with Thagard's work. They suggest that jurors attempt to make up coherent stories to account for the facts. This has implications for the order in which evidence is presented. Rather than putting your strongest evidence first or last, the evidence for your theory should be presented in the sequence of the unfolding mechanism in your theory.

Bucking the Zeitgeist

Presenting a new idea or way of thinking about some phenomenon to consumers who already have a favored explanation is often difficult. Lee Ross, Mark Lepper, and their colleagues have shown very clearly what one is up against. In their work on belief perseverance, Ross, Lepper, and Hubbard (1979) demonstrated that even when the evidence on which a theory was constructed is credibly discredited, individuals tend to cling to the original theory (see also Anderson, Lepper, & Ross, 1980). One of the most dramatic demonstrations of this kind of phenomenon was presented by Lord, Ross, and Lepper (1979). They provided advocates on two sides of a particular position with research summaries that either supported or contradicted their point of view. Advocates rated the studies that agreed with them as more convincing and those that disagreed with them as less convincing. What is astonishing is that even after reading the research summary that contradicted their position, advocates became more polarized in their point of view!

The literature on scripts (Schank & Abelson, 1977), schemas (e.g., Smith, 1998), frames, and so on, suggest that when something new is encountered, there is a strong tendency to assimilate it to one's already available schema. When confronting a new theoretical point of view, there is a tendency to see it as simply a "warmed over" version of or a simple variation of "XYZ" theory. Aspects of the new theory that inevitably remain unstated will be filled in with the defaults from XYZ theory. Small, subtle deviations from XYZ theory will be assimilated to look more like XYZ theory. On the other hand, a clear inconsistency with XYZ theory will tend to be particularly well remembered (Hastie & Kumar, 1979) and more deeply processed (Clary & Tesser, 1983).

If one's new theory is so dramatically different from what has come before, consumers will approach understanding it in a piecemeal fashion (Fiske & Neuberg, 1988). Each proposition will be individually evaluated in forming an impression of it. But the pieces are not likely to be very memorable without some kind of cognitive organization within which to fit it.

New ways of looking at and interpreting the world are difficult to get accepted, but they sometimes do get established. All of the S-ideas I mentioned were once new. How did they get established? Clearly there are idiosyncratic features associated with each case but research by Serge Moscovici (e.g., 1980) suggests that it is possible to change the zeitgeist. According to this research, for a new theory to be accepted, it must be presented consistently, without concession to the zeitgeist point of view. Whereas zeitgeist-related work tends to be accepted without deep processing, a consistently presented new point of view will occasion new and often creative thinking (Nemeth, 1986) among potential consumers. Indeed, outright adoption of the new idea may be less likely than changes in receptivity to related ideas. What all this suggests is that if you are convinced that you have an important new way of looking at the world, don't compromise and don't give up!

A SUMMING UP

Almost all consumers of research agree on the importance of theory. This chapter focused on impactful theories and hypotheses. The two aspects of impact that received the most attention are the interest value of the idea and the credibility of the idea. After reviewing some interesting theories and hypotheses, I discussed heuristics for generating interesting ideas. The discussion suggested that the factors that affect credibility or the acceptance of an idea depend on whether the idea is totally new or contradicts the zeitgeist.

REFERENCES

Abelson, R. P. (1995). *Statistics as principled argument*. Hillsdale, NJ: Erlbaum.

Adorno, T. W., Frenkel-Brunswik, E., Levinson, D. J., & Sanford, R. N. (1950). *The authoritarian personality*. New York: Harper & Row.

Ainsworth, M. D. S., Blehar, M. C., Waters, E., & Wall, S. (1978). *Patterns of attachment: A psychological study of the strange situation*. Hillsdale, NJ: Erlbaum.

Allport, F. M. (1920). The influence of the group upon association and thought. *Journal of Experimental Psychology, 3*, 159–182.

Anderson, C. A., Lepper, M. R., & Ross, L. (1980). Perseverance of social theories: The role of explanation in the persistence of discredited information. *Journal of Personality and Social Psychology, 39*, 1037–1049.

Aron, A., & Aron, E. N. (1986). *The heart of social psychology*, Lexington, MA: Lexington Books.

Aronson, E., Wilson, T. D. & Brewer, M. B. (1998). Experimentation in social psychology. In D. T. Gilbert, S. T. Fiske, & G. Lindzey (Eds.), *The handbook of social psychology* (Vol. 1, 4th ed., pp. 99–142). Boston: McGraw-Hill.

Asch, S. E. (1956). Studies of independence and conformity: A minority of one against a unanimous majority. *Psychological Monographs, 70*, 416.

Bem, D. J. (1965). An experimental analysis of self-persuasion. *Journal of Experimental Social Psychology, 1*, 199–218.

Bem, D. J. (1967). Self-perception: An alternative interpretation of cognitive dissonance phenomena. *Psychological Review, 74*, 183–200.

Bem, D. J. (1972). Self-perception theory: In L. Berkowitz (Ed.), *Advances in experimental social psychology* (Vol. 6). New York: Academic Press.

Berglas, S., & Jones, E. E. (1978). Drug choice as a self-handicapping strategy in response to noncontingent success. *Journal of Personality and Social Psychology, 36*, 405–417.

Berscheid, E., & Walster (Hatfield), E. (1978). *Interpersonal attraction*. Reading, MA: Addison-Wesley.

Chaiken, S. (1987). The heuristic model of persuasion. In M. P. Zanna, J. M. Olson, & C. P. Herman (Eds.), *Social influence: The Ontario Symposium* (Vol. 5, pp. 3–39). Hillsdale, NJ: Erlbaum.

Cialdini, R. B. (1985). *Influence: Science and practice*. Glenview, IL: Scott Foresman.

Cialdini, R. B., Borden, R. J., Thorne, A., Walker, M. R., Freeman, S., & Sloan, L. R. (1976). Basking in reflected glory: Three (football) field studies. *Journal of Personality and Social Psychology, 34*, 366–375.

Clary, E. G., & Tesser, A. (1983). Reactions to unexpected events: The naive scientist and interpretive activity. *Personality and Social Psychology Bulletin, 9*, 609–620.

Csikszentmihalyi, M. (1982). Toward a psychology of optimal experience. In L. Wheeler (Ed.), *Review of personality and social psychology* (Vol. 3, pp. 13–36). Beverly Hills, CA: Sage.

Darley, J. M., & Latané, B. (1968, December). When will people help in a crisis? *Psychology Today*, pp. 54–57, 70–71.

Deci, E. L. (1971). Effects of externally mediated rewards on intrinsic motivation. *Journal of Personality and Social Psychology, 18,* 105–115.

Festinger, L. (1957). *A theory of cognitive dissonance.* Stanford, CA: Stanford University Press.

Festinger L., & Carlsmith, J. M. (1959). Cognitive consequences of forced compliance. *Journal of Abnormal and Social Psychology, 58,* 203–210.

Fiske, S. T., & Neuberg, S. L. (1988). A continuum model of impression formation: From category-based to individuating processes as a function of information, motivation, and attention. *Advances in Experimental Social Psychology, 23,* 1–108.

Gleick, J. (1987). *Chaos: Making a new science.* New York: Viking.

Hastie, R., & Kumar, P. (1979). Person memory: Personality traits as organizing principles in memory for behaviors. *Journal of Personality and Social Psychology, 37,* 25–38.

Hazan, C., & Shaver, P. (1987). Romantic love conceptualized as an attachment process. *Journal of Personality and Social Psychology, 52,* 511–524.

Heider, F. (1958). *The psychology of interpersonal relations.* New York: Wiley.

Higgins, E. T. (1987). Self-discrepancy: A theory relating self and affect. *Psychological Review, 94,* 319–340.

Jones, R. A. (1985). *Research methods in the social and behavioral sciences.* Sunderland, MA: Sinauer Associates.

Kelley, H. H. (1973). The processes of causal attribution. *American Psychologist, 28,* 103–128.

Latané, B., & Darley, J. M. (1970). *The unresponsive bystander: Why doesn't he help.* New York, Appleton-Century-Crofts.

Lecky, P. (1945). *Self-consistency; A theory of personality.* New York: Island Press.

Lepper, M. R., Greene, D., & Nisbett, R. E. (1973). Undermining children's intrinsic interest with extrinsic reward: A test of the "overjustification" hypothesis. *Journal of Personality and Social Psychology, 28,* 129–137.

Lord, C. G., Ross, L., & Leppei, M. R. (1979). Biased assimilation and attitude polarization: The effects of prior theories on subsequently considered evidence. *Journal of Personality and Social Psychology, 37,* 2098–2109.

McGuire, W. J. (1973). The Yin and Yang of progress in social psychology: *Seven Koan. Journal of Personality and Social Psychology, 26,* 446–456.

McGuire, W. J. (1983). A contextualist theory of knowledge: Its implications for innovation and reform in psychological research. In L. Berkowitz (Ed.), *Advances in experimental social psychology* (Vol. 16, pp. 1–47). New York: Academic Press.

McGuire, W. J. (1997). Creative hypothesis generating in psychology: Some useful heuristics. *Annual Review of Psychology, 48,* 1–30.

Milgram, S. (1974). *Obedience to authority: An experimental view.* New York: Harper & Row.

Moray, N. (1959). Attention in dichotic listening. Affective cues and the influence of instructions. *Quarterly Journal of Experimental Psychology, 11,* 56–60.

Moscovici, S. (1980). Toward a theory of conversion behavior. In L. Berkowitz (Ed.), *Advances in experimental social psychology* (Vol. 13, pp. 209–239). New York: Academic Press.

Nemeth, C. J. (1986). Differential contributions of majority and minority influence. *Psychological Review, 93,* 23–32.

Nowak, A., Szamrej, J., & Latane, B. (1990). From private attitude to public opinion: A dynamic theory of social impact. *Psychological Review, 97,* 362–376.

Pennington, N., & Hastie, R. (1992). Explaining the evidence: Tests of the story model for juror decision making. *Journal of Personality and Social Psychology, 62,* 189–206.

Pessin, J. (1933). The comparative effects of social and mechanical stimulation on memorizing. *American Journal of Psychology, 45,* 263–270.

Petty, R. E., & Cacioppo, J. T. (1986). The elaboration likelihood model of persuasion. In L. Berkowitz (Ed.), *Advances in Experimental Social Psychology, 19,* 123–181.

Read, S. J., & Marcus-Newhall, A. (1993). Explanatory coherence in social explanations: A parallel distributed processing account. *Journal of Personality and Social Psychology, 65,* 429–447.

Rogers, C. A. (1961). *On becoming a person.* New York: Houghton-Mifflin.

Rosnow, R. L. (1991). Inside rumor: A personal journey. *American Psychologist, 46,* 484–496.

Ross, L., Lepper, M. R., & Hubbard, M. (1979). Perseverance in self perception and social perception: Biased attributional processes in the debriefing paradigm. *Journal of Personality and Social Psychology, 32,* 880–892.

Rotter, J. B. (1966). Generalized expectancies for internal versus external control of reinforcement. *Psychological Monographs, 80,* (1, Whole No. 609).

Salovey, P., & Rodin, J. (1984). Some antecedents and consequences of social-comparison jealousy. *Journal of Personality and Social Psychology, 47,* 780–792.

Schank, R., & Abelson, R. (1977). *Scripts, plans, goals and understanding.* Hillsdale, NJ: Erlbaum.

Simonton, D. K. (1985). Quality, quantity and age: The careers of ten distinguished psychologists. *International Journal of Aging and Human Development, 21,* 241–254.

Smith, E. R. (1998). Mental representation and memory. In D. T. Gilbert, S. T. Fiske, & G. Lindzey (Eds.) *The handbook of social psychology* (Vol. 1, 4th ed. pp. 391–445). Boston: McGraw-Hill.

Spence, K. W., Farber, I. E., & McFann, H. H. (1956). The relation of anxiety (drive) level to performance in competitional and non-competitional paired associates learning. *Journal of Experimental Psychology, 52,* 296–305.

Steele, C. M. (1988). The psychology of self-affirmation: Sustaining the integrity of self. In L. Berkowitz (Ed.), *Advances in Experimental Social Psychology* (Vol. 21, pp. 261–302). New York: Academic Press.

Strunk, W., & White, E. B. (1959). *The elements of style.* New York: Macmillan.

Swann, W. B. (1983). Self-verification: Bringing social reality into harmony with the self. In J. Suls & A. G. Greenwald (Eds.) *Psychological perspectives on the self* (Vol. 2). Hillsdale, NJ: Erlbaum.

Tedeschi, J. T., Schlenker, B. R., & Bonoma, T. V. (1971). Cognitive dissonance: Private ratiocination or public spectacle? *American Psychologist, 26,* 685–695.

Tesser, A. (1988). Toward a self-evaluation maintenance model of social behavior. In L. Berkowitz (Ed.), *Advances in experimental social psychology* (Vol. 21, pp. 181–227). New York: Academic Press.

Tesser, A. (1990, August). Interesting models in social psychology: A personal view. Invited address presented at the annual meeting of the American Psychological Association, Boston, MA.

Thagard, P. (1989). Explanatory coherence. *Behavioral and Brain Sciences, 12,* 435–467.

Travis, L. E. (1925). The effect of a small audience upon eye-hand coordination. *Journal of Abnormal and Social Psychology, 20,* 142–146.

Triplett,, N. (1898). The dynamogenic factors in pacemaking and competition. *American Journal of Psychology, 9,* 507–533.

Weick, K. E. (1989). Theory construction as disciplined imagination. *Academy of Management Review, 14,* 516–531.

Wicklund, R. (1986). Orientation to the environment versus preoccupation with human potential. In R. M. Sorrentino, & E. T. Higgins (Eds.), *Handbook of motivation and cognition: Foundations of social behavior.* (pp. 64–95). New York: Guilford.

Zajonc, R. B. (1965). Social facilitation. *Science, 149,* 269–274.

Zillman, D., & Bryant, J. (Eds.). (1985). *Selective exposure to communication.* Hillsdale, NJ: Erlbaum.

Chapter 6

Writing Effectively about Design

HARRY T. REIS

L et's face it. Not many of us look forward to curling up in bed
late at night with a spellbinding design section. Although
dedicated aficionados of the art of psychological research may be
enthralled by clever, creative designs, most of us would rather
reserve our passion for theory and data. In the family hierarchy of
the psychology research article, experimental design resembles the
poor cousin who must be invited to the party but is never the guest
of honor.

This situation is in some ways unfortunate. At first glance, focusing on the well-written experimental design section is analogous to
describing a new car in terms of the mechanical design of the engine.
Engine specifications are what make the car work, but rarely does
one leave the showroom excited about engine mechanics.
Nevertheless, with a flawed design, the car will sputter and die, but a
vehicle with a well-structured engine will keep its passengers sailing
smoothly in pursuit of their goals. And so it goes with experimental
design. A flawed design will derail even the most impressive theory
and hypotheses, whereas appropriate, well-thought-out designs usually lead to informative research and compelling findings.

For this reason, the design section of a psychology journal article
may be its most important and informative section. Nearly everything
else in the article depends on it. With a design firmly in mind, and
some rudimentary knowledge of the literature, experienced readers
(such as journal reviewers) can usually discern a study's potential theoretical contribution. Design also dictates many features of method

and data analysis. Perhaps most important, design more than any other quality (except the data themselves, of course) determines what conclusions can and cannot be drawn. For these reasons, critical (and experienced) readers often look first at the design section to see if there are obvious alternative explanations, and to see if the design matches the theoretical issues raised in the introduction. It is apparent, in short, that developing a good experimental design and describing it clearly and informatively is an essential step in writing an effective and influential article.

Design statements in contemporary psychological research are considerably more diverse and multifaceted than they were one or two decades ago. Whereas designs were once limited in common practice to minor variations on the theme of factorial analysis of variance, the available options are now far wider. They include, for example, quasi-experiments such as regression discontinuity and interrupted time series designs; multilevel modeling; single-sample structure methods such as multidimensional scaling, cluster analysis, and covariance structure models; mathematical modeling; and temporal methods such as time series and growth curve analysis. The good news is that the field's enlarged repertoire of strategies for studying behavior has, as seems likely to continue, enhanced the validity and usefulness of its findings. The less-than-good news is that because one's audience is less likely to be fully conversant with any given design or method, more information needs to be provided in a research report. In short, the premium for effective writing is expanding, and seems likely to continue to grow in importance.

WHY DESIGN MATTERS IN A RESEARCH REPORT

The design section of a research article sets forth a blueprint of operations by which one or more theory-based propositions were transformed into an empirical study composed either of systematically varied conditions (in the case of experiments and quasi-experiments) or of a series of variables to be correlated. Design also includes information about subjects' participation in the study – whether they participated in one or several conditions, for example, and whether they were randomly assigned to conditions. The Design section differs from the Procedure section in that the latter is concerned with procedural details of what was done; the former describes the conceptual layout of constructs into conditions and variables.

A research design provides more than an outline of how a study was conducted, however; it sets boundaries for the kind of conclusions that can be drawn from the data. There are several reasons why design circumscribes one's conclusions, the most important of which is that a given design enhances the plausibility of certain interpretations while diminishing others. Because the goal in writing any research report is not just to communicate one's findings, but also to argue for the validity of particular explanations, it is imperative to show how a study's design is appropriate for supporting the theories and hypotheses being investigated.

Sternberg and Gordeeva (1996) asked a sample of experienced researchers to rate the importance of 45 attributes in determining the impact of an article on the field. The highest-ranked item was "Makes an obvious contribution to psychological knowledge, adding something new and substantial." Although many factors contribute to such impact, the right experimental design is indispensable. Without it, alternative explanations and conceptual ambiguities are likely to pose significant challenges to preferred theoretical accounts. With it, no other interpretation of the data will be as plausible as the principles that suggested your research in the first place.

One way in which research designs influence validity is by ensuring that the most relevant comparisons are included. For example, suppose a researcher wanted to demonstrate that upward social comparison (comparison to better-off others) had detrimental effects on psychological well-being, whereas downward comparison (comparison to worse-off others) was beneficial. Simply contrasting these two conditions would be somewhat ambiguous, because even the hypothesized result would leave begging the question of whether upward comparison had a negative effect, downward comparison had a positive effect, or both. A three-group design, adding a comparison-to-equals condition, would distinguish among these three potential explanations. Often, more than one extra comparison group may be needed. For example, in clinical psychology, the efficacy of an intervention is best established by comparing individuals in the focal treatment not only with others not receiving treatment, but also with people seeking but not receiving treatment (i.e., a waiting-list control group) and people in superficially similar programs that lack the hypothesized active agent of the intervention (i.e., an attention-control group).

Another way in which research designs foster valid inference is by eliminating the possibility of confounds. As Crano and Brewer point out, "the design of experiments should be oriented toward eliminating possible explanations of research results . . . which are unrelated to the effects of the treatment (independent variable) of interest" (1973, p. 27). Consider the hypothesis that people learn faster when their subject matter is freely chosen rather than forced. One group of participants is allowed to choose which of several computer games to learn; another group is assigned games randomly. A subtle but plausible confound is that the chosen puzzles may be more interesting, user-friendly, or easier, so that faster learning, if it occurs, may reflect characteristics of desirable games rather than the context of learning. A better design rules out this alternative by yoking, that is, by having participants in both groups attempt the same games.

Random assignment of participants to conditions is also an important feature of good experimental designs (although this is not possible for variables that cannot be manipulated, such as sex, age, or intellectual ability). When participants are not assigned randomly, the obtained results may reflect the basis of assignment to conditions rather than the manipulation. Because alternative explanations of this sort inevitably weaken the case for a particular causal interpretation, most researchers generally prefer designs using random assignment whenever it is reasonable to do so.

Whatever the merits and disadvantages of a given research design, it is certain that reviewers and skeptically minded readers will focus on them in deciding whether your research actually supports the conclusions you favor. Therefore, novices should resist the temptation to reserve their best writing for the theory sections of a report. A well-written, persuasive description of design is often crucial to making those theoretical contributions clear.

HOW TO WRITE ABOUT RESEARCH DESIGNS

There is, of course, a world of difference between having a good research design and writing effectively about it. Influential articles require, first, a well-crafted design that is appropriate to the topic under investigation; and, second, evidence to this effect in the written report. Like a good map, a research design write-up should illuminate connections between one's point of departure (theory) and destination (findings), so that the reader's path is free of dead ends, detours, and wrong turns. To do this, most researchers include an explicit one- or two-sentence overview of their design at the beginning of the methods section. Sometimes this overview appears in the final paragraph of the introduction. This description should not come as a surprise, however; the rationale for a study, as presented in the introduction, should move smoothly and informatively from concepts to operations, so that the design statement is more or less redundant by the time it appears.

In general terms, a well-written discussion of design should follow the three *c*s: *clear, comprehensive,* and *compelling.* Clarity is important because an unnecessarily complex or oblique discussion may confuse or disorient readers just when you most want them following your logic: how your conceptualization of a problem leads to the specific research that you conducted. Consider the following example:

There were four groups in this experiment. Participants in one group were led to expect success on a task described as important to their self-concept. Another group anticipated poor performance, but the task was less personally relevant. The third group expected to do well, but felt that the task was not ego-involving, whereas the final group was personally involved and expected to fail.

Contrast the above with:

Subjects were randomly assigned to one cell of a 2 (anticipated outcome) × 2 (level of ego-involvement) design. Half of the participants were led to expect success, whereas the other half were led to expect failure. Within each of these conditions, half of the participants engaged in an ego-involving task; for the other half, the task was not ego-involving.

The second statement is clearer and more concise. It makes obvious that the design was a 2 × 2 between-groups factorial (see below), that the independent variables were anticipated outcome and ego-involvement, and that random assignment was used. Readers of the first paragraph may eventually reach the same conclusion, or they may not.

Design statements also lose clarity when they are overly eloquent or verbose rather than succinct. Compare:

All of the individuals who agreed to take part in this research were assigned very, very carefully to either the positive or negative feedback condition in much the manner that a child might disperse petals of a daisy when playing "she loves me, she loves me not."

with:

Participants were alternately assigned to the positive and negative feedback conditions.

The best design descriptions are short and to the point. Beware of overkill. The theoretical rationale for your design should have been made clear earlier, and there is no need to provide a primer on the general benefits of factorial designs or random assignment (unless your study presents unusual issues). If your design is very complex – but only then – an illustrative figure may be helpful. Regarding language, there may be a time and place for metaphor and evocative adverbs within a research report, but they are distracting and annoying when presenting a design. Display your creative writing talents elsewhere. Elegance here is a function of brevity, clarity, and thoroughness. Readers may not notice the beauty of your words in a well-written design section, but they are more likely to be impressed by the lucidity of your research.

The second quality of an effective description of design, comprehensiveness, refers to the inclusion of all relevant material that readers expect to find. Like any good organizational scheme, American Psychological Association (APA) style promotes efficiency, and there is certain information that experienced readers look for in a design statement. Although every study and design requires at least somewhat unique information (as described in the next section), the following general questions pertain to most research reports[1].

---

[1] With multistudy papers rapidly becoming the norm in some areas of psychology, which use similar designs for more than one study, it is usually expeditious to use the first study as a template for describing subsequent studies, detailing only their new features.

1. *Design.* What type of design was used? Was it experimental, quasi-experimental, or correlational? How many factors were there with how many levels? Were they varied between-participants or within-participants? Were nesting or multiple assessments used, and if so, were there controls for order (counterbalancing)? Normally, designs are not referenced, although the more unfamiliar a design within a research area, the more helpful one or two general references may be.

2. *Participant assignment.* On what basis were participants distributed across conditions?

3. *Independent variable(s).* What was the independent variable and how (by which conditions) was it represented? What relevant features of the research environment were controlled?

4. *Dependent variable(s).* On what variables was the impact of the independent variable assessed?

If nothing else, making these points crystal clear ensures that readers will not misperceive your work. As essential as it is for readers to understand what you did, however, the most compelling papers also ensure that readers appreciate why you did your research in that manner. Because there is invariably more than one way to investigate most questions in psychology, it is important to make plain how the particular design you used embodies the contrasts and comparisons that your theory specifies. Researchers often choose one design over another for reasons that are not self-evident, in which case readers (who cannot be faulted for knowing less about the problem than you do, or for approaching it from a different vantage point) may assume that other designs might have been preferable or that critical control conditions are missing. Even when a study is not hypothesis-testing in nature – it may be exploratory or hypothesis-generating – there should be a clearly articulated rationale for its design.

Try to take the perspective of an outsider to your research. Is it clear why these conditions are appropriate for examining your hypotheses? Can plausible alternative explanations be discounted with these conditions, control groups, and measures? What are the specific advantages of this design over other reasonable possibilities, especially those that have been used in prior research? (But remember that modesty is called for. Science often progresses in slow steps, and it is likely that your paper will be read, if not reviewed, by the authors of those prior papers.) If there are multiple control groups (as in the intervention example above), what is the function of each one? Do any conditions, groups, or assessments seem superfluous? What are the limitations, if any, of your design? (Noting limitations, usually done in the discussion section, is a useful way to avoid drawing stronger conclusions than the results can bear.) Answers to these questions should be evident even to a casual reader.

The rationale for a design is not typically reported in the design statement of a methods section, which generally does no more than provide an explicit summary. Rather, it should be developed throughout the introduction, as the text progresses from general discussion of theoretical principles to specific hypotheses. A good way to do this is to be clear about design considerations as you discuss prior research, especially your own studies that used similar designs. For example, one might note that a prior study contrasted condition A with condition B in order to rule out a particular alternative explanation, but that now a different comparison is called for. The more compelling the case that a design can unequivocally support a given theoretical position while refuting plausible alternatives, the more likely it is that an article will be reviewed favorably, and the greater its likely impact on the field.

There is nothing like an unambiguous, clearly specified design to enhance the comprehensibility of results. An appropriate, concise design lets readers anticipate the data analyses that follow, and gives them a useful framework for following the detailed presentation of data analyses into general conclusions. To be sure, design does not dictate statistics – research questions do – but design represents those questions in concrete terms and can make results more accessible to readers, in much the same way that a well-crafted table or figure can be assimilated more easily than prose results can. The more complex a study or its results, the more helpful is this additional level of clarity.

BASIC DESIGNS AND WHAT TO SAY ABOUT THEM

Psychological research is a lot more complex than it once was. Whereas in the not too distant past a few basic designs sufficed for most questions, the accumulation of a sizable literature and growing technical complexity of the field has dictated that contemporary researchers develop and become familiar with diverse designs (Reis & Stiller, 1992). Thus, whereas it once might have been possible to fully describe and explain a standard research design with one or two phrases, a bit more attention is now needed. Any basic research methods textbook explains the advantages and disadvantages of most of these designs. What is not as readily apparent, given their complexity and diversity, is how to convey the essential features of a given design clearly yet efficiently.

Although there are similarities, each type of design necessitates its own specifications. Consequently, the information contained in the ideal description varies from one design to another. Here are some guideposts about the details that most readers expect to find.

Between-Participants Experimental Designs

Experimental designs are between-participants, within-participants, or mixed. In a between design, all participants take part in one and only one cell of the design, whereas in the latter (discussed under the next heading) the same participants engage in multiple conditions. Between-participant designs require mention of how participants were assigned to conditions – randomly or by some other procedure. If the former, it is typically not necessary to explain how this was accomplished, but if the latter, explanation is usually desirable.

In these designs, experimental conditions are specified according to the independent variables (IV). Each IV has two or more conditions (or levels). If there is more than one IV, the design is called a factorial design. It is common to refer to factorial designs by the number of levels of each IV (or factor). For example, a $3 \times 2 \times 2$ factorial design has three IVs, one with three levels and two with two levels each, resulting in 12 combinations (or cells). Design statements should always be clear about the IVs, the levels of each IV, and the factorial structure that organized them, which may not be apparent. For example, a study with four different treatment groups might have a 2×2 design, or one IV with four levels. Design statements are also clarified by naming the variables along with the number of levels: for example, a 3 (learning condition) $\times$ 2 (instructional medium) $\times$ 2 (level of difficulty) design.

Experiments with a single dependent variable (DV) are called univariate, whereas those with multiple DVs are called multivariate. In
multivariate designs, it is generally useful to describe how the DVs
are organized, for example, whether they assess separate constructs
or are essentially parallel.

Within-Participants and Mixed Designs

If the same persons participated in more than one condition, the
design is said to be within-participant (the terms nested, blocked, and
repeated measures are also common); for example, each subject might
engage in a perceptual discrimination task under several different conditions. Within-subject designs are often employed to permit a more
sensitive test of a treatment effect by reducing error variance associated with individual differences. The structure of IVs (factorial, etc.) in
these designs is described in the same way as in between-participant
designs. Thus, a 2×2 within-participant study means that each participant provided data for each of the four combinations of two independent variables. But because each individual engaged in multiple
conditions, order of administration is almost sure to be important (e.g.,
fatigue, learning, or reactivity are likely) and should be clear in your
write-up. Common strategies for contending with order effects include
counterbalancing (i.e., an equal number of participants experience
each condition in each serial position), partial randomization (in
which only certain orderings, chosen to control for the most plausible
effects, are used), and randomization, as well as leaving order fixed. If
your strategy for dealing with order effects involves adding one or
more IVs (representing order) to the design, these variables should
generally be treated as design variables in their own right. For example,
in the case of counterbalancing (which necessarily turns a repeated
measures design into a mixed design; see below):

A 2 (method of instruction) $\times$ 2 (order of presentation) repeated measures
design was used, with half of the subjects randomly assigned to receive computerized instruction first; the other half received face-to-face instruction first.

Because order of presentation, if left uncontrolled, is a common
source of mundane alternative explanations (e.g., subjects may perform better on a second task not because of the manipulation but

because they were more familiar with the task), it should be discussed prominently in describing your design.

Designs that include at least one between-participants and one within-participants independent variable are called mixed designs. In a mixed design, information about assignment (for the between portion of the design) and order of administration (for the within portion) is needed. Here is a description of a hypothetical mixed design that contains all of the relevant elements:

Participants were randomly assigned to one of two conditions. In the *fast-learning* condition, they were shown slides of 100 faces each exposed for 1 second; in the *slow-learning* condition, the same slides were exposed for 3 seconds each. Following a 5-minute delay, all participants were tested for recall. The order in which male and female faces were shown was counterbalanced, with some participants seeing the 50 male faces first and others seeing the 50 female faces first. Thus, a 2 (speed of learning) × 2 (facial sex) × 2 (male faces first – female faces first) mixed design was used, with repeated measures on the latter two factors.

There is little ambiguity about experimental design in this paragraph. Of course, a rationale is needed, which should have been supplied in the introduction, as are details about how the faces were photographed and presented, the recall assessment, and other features essential to operationalizing the design. This material should follow in the methods section; the clear design statement allows readers to anticipate the details that follow.

The benefit of a within design is not limited to persons. Just as error variance may be reduced by employing the same individuals in multiple treatment groups, error variance may also be diminished by pairing individuals whose performance is likely to be correlated. For example, in a study of marital satisfaction, the IV of sex is within-couple, because a husband's and wife's satisfaction is likely to be correlated. Participants may also be matched according to important background variables (e.g., IQ in learning experiments, or preexisting levels of aggressivity in a behavior intervention study). A special case of nesting is called *yoking*, in which stimulus materials for participants in one condition are matched to those chosen by participants in another condition, in order to control for activity differences. For example, in the earlier computer game example, intrinsic differences in game content are controlled by exposing participants in the forced-choice condition to the same games chosen by free-choice participants. Within-unit designs are a valuable strategy for increasing power in psychological research, although, as noted above, they may add complications to a design. Consequently, design statements should be clear not only about the basis for repeated measures or nesting, but also about controls for order and reactivity.

More Complex Within-Participant Designs

Designs involving repeated assessment of the same individuals over time have become increasingly popular in several areas of psychological research. In developmental psychology, longitudinal studies examine patterns of change and consistency across time spans as long as a lifetime. Daily event studies examine behavior, thought, and emotion in natural contexts by repeated collection of diary-like records over varying intervals, such as several times during a day or every day for several months (Reis & Gable, in press). Time-series designs investigate sequential change from one observation to the next, typically over many closely spaced intervals. In these and other similar designs, employing numerous within-person observations allows investigators to address hypotheses about variability and change with greater precision than that afforded by standard methods.

Describing these designs in journal format requires clear information about the units of assessment. How many data collections were there for each individual, and how were they spaced? (Irregular intervals or inconsistent schedules from one participant to another usually create problems for data analysis and interpretation.) If the intervals are close in time, is there any possibility of overlap or confounding? Attrition is always a problem in longitudinal designs; what steps were taken to minimize attrition and/or examine its impact? Likewise, with many assessments, at least a small amount of missing data is inevitable; how was this problem addressed? Perhaps most important, because statistical methods for these designs can be highly specialized, descriptions of a design may be more informative if aligned with consideration of the appropriateness of a method for a particular data set. For example, time-series designs are usually clearer if the method for examining trends and patterns across time is specified.

As may be apparent, the further a researcher moves from the standard of between-participants experimental designs, the more idiosyncratic are the design statements. These designs seem likely to become ever more commonplace in psychological research. Nevertheless, although the essential details may vary, the rules for writing an effective design statement remain constant: be clear, comprehensive, and compelling. In fact, if anything, as the field's methodological diversity grows, the value of a persuasive, well-written description of design is likely to expand accordingly.

Quasi-Experiments

Quasi-experiments are studies in which random assignment to conditions is not carried out, usually because it is impossible or impractical; instead, explicit steps are taken to control for alternative explanations associated with the grouping of participants into conditions (Cook & Campbell, 1979; West, Biesanz, & Pitts, in press). The most common quasi-experimental design in psychology is the *nonequivalent control group* design, which contrasts groups differing in some treatment or naturally occurring event. For example, one might compare the postgraduate success of science and nonscience majors; recidivism among prisoners who do and do not participate in educational programs; or emotional well-being among victims and nonvictims of natural disasters. Quasi-experiments differ from true experiments in that participants are not randomly assigned to treatments, but they differ from correlational studies by incorporating procedures to examine and control for preexisting differences between groups. Most typically this involves pre- and postmeasurement, or assessment of related background variables (called covariates), so that the treatment groups can be equated statistically. In the postgraduate success case, for example, one might attempt to rule out other predictors of postgraduate success by controlling for SAT scores and socioeconomic background.

Structurally, quasi-experimental designs can be described in terms quite similar to those used in randomized multiple group experiments, with additional information on the procedures adopted to evaluate and control alternative explanations. Because quasi-experimental methods are not as well known as randomized experiments, researchers should describe their designs carefully, with particular attention to internal validity[2]. For example, in the nonequivalent control group design, the rationale for specific covariates and how they will be employed should be explicit. In another common quasi-experiment, the interrupted time series design, which examines trends across several measurements before and after an event, the timing of intervals should be discussed, as well as controls for the possibility of extraneous occurrences. Most important, the design and controls should be matched to the most plausible alternative explanations.

Although quasi-experiments are unlikely to replace randomized experiments in the programs of researchers committed to definitive demonstrations of causality, their ability to examine causal hypotheses absent of randomization makes them increasingly popular for field research, for generalizing causal principles outside controlled laboratory conditions, and for evaluating the impact of naturally occurring events and interventions. The uniqueness of quasi-experimental design places a premium on clarity. If your design is presented clearly and compellingly, readers will be in the best position to gauge the success of your research in supporting your preferred explanation over alternatives.

Correlational Designs

Correlational designs are based on measured, as opposed to manipulated, variables, and therefore are generally not used for testing causal hypotheses. Nevertheless, correlational designs often yield important findings that contribute to the field's understanding of behavior. Furthermore, because certain variables cannot be manipulated, such as sex, intellectual or athletic ability, national origin or residence, and personality, they can only be studied correlationally. Isolating, identifying, and clarifying patterns of association among variables, the major functions of correlational methods, are therefore necessary and desirable strategies in many areas of psychological research.

---

[2] Internal validity refers to the confidence with which the obtained results can be attributed to the IV, as opposed to some other factor associated with it.

When writing about correlational research, it is important to avoid confusing correlational designs and correlational statistics. Statistical methods such as analysis of variance (ANOVA) and correlation-regression analysis are essentially identical from a mathematical standpoint (Cohen & Cohen, 1983), so it is erroneous to assume that the former permits causal inference whereas the latter does not. Causality is a property occasioned by experimental design – randomization and manipulation – rather than a method of statistical analysis. Consequently, design statements should be clear about the kinds of inferences that a particular study can and cannot support.

Diverse and highly sophisticated correlational methods are rapidly becoming standard fare in psychological research. For example, hierarchical regression analysis permits separation and independent scrutiny of variance components representing distinct hypotheses and processes; techniques such as factor analysis, cluster analysis, and multidimensional scaling can help identify underlying structural organization within complex systems of variables; and covariance structure methods, such as structural equation modeling, allow researchers to evaluate how well a given data set fits several alternative theoretical models (see Wegener & Fabrigar, in press, for an overview of these methods). When these techniques are used for theory-testing purposes, as they are increasingly, it is desirable to specify a conceptual model in advance, often in the form of a diagram, so that theory-testing results can be distinguished from post hoc data fitting.

Given the extensive array of correlational strategies and techniques, the prime consideration in writing a design section is defining the procedure and illuminating its affinity to the questions under scrutiny and the data being analyzed. Although design presentation should not become a discussion of statistical technique, it is important to show how the study fits the method. Correlational methods applied ambiguously or seemingly chosen more for convenience than appropriateness are unlikely to tell a convincing story about substantive findings. Be sure to describe carefully how all variables relate to the overall analytic design, and be clear in showing that their relative role is determined not by chance (always a concern with many correlational variables!), but by a well-articulated theory-driven plan. In addition, the various methods each have their own design criteria and conventions that readers will need to know. For example, some correlational designs permit comparison of the pattern of correlation among variables across several groups. Other designs involve multiple stages and steps. The likelihood that most readers will have at best passing familiarity with your methods makes the three cs – to be clear, comprehensive, and compelling – all the more important.

CONCLUSION: WRITING FOR IMPACT ABOUT DESIGN

From a literary standpoint, design sections are among the easier, if not the easiest, parts of a journal article to write. Aside from making your statements clear, comprehensive, and compelling, there's little more that needs to be said. Literary simplicity should not be confused with import, however; the design section is critical, leaving little room for error or omission. The importance of elegant, creative, and timely theorizing notwithstanding, behavioral science at its core is all about the evidence, and how well it supports a given set of principles. Such support is a direct consequence of research design. Good designs provide a strong foundation for the validity of conclusions by fostering particular explanations and ruling out others. Poor designs are either inappropriate to the conclusions or invite conceptual ambiguity. In short, the extent to which a study adds to knowledge depends as much on design as anything else.

Strategically, to have one's research published in top journals, design is vital. Design statements often stand out in impact relative to their small number of words. My experience as an editor and reviewer suggests that the first question reviewers (and other readers) ask is whether the obtained results of a study validly and unambiguously lead to the conceptual conclusions that an author advocates. If the answer is no, or even maybe not, reviewers are likely to raise substantial questions about a paper's contribution to the literature, irrespective of its theoretical polish and numerous highly significant results. Design is a big part of that judgment (although certainly not the only part) and it is therefore generally a good idea to prepare a design section with skeptical reviewers in mind.

Having a good research design but writing poorly about it is like painting a beautiful work of art and then exhibiting it behind an opaque screen. The work may be inherently excellent and important, but no one is likely to know about it. And unlike works of art, which are sometimes created for the artist's private enjoyment, research needs to be publicized if it is to influence future research and applications by others. Thus, although design sections may not cast a spell that inspires bedtime enthusiasm, their impact is unmistakable.

ACKNOWLEDGMENTS

For their very helpful comments and suggestions I am grateful to Arthur Aron, Shelly Gable, and Richard Gramzow.

REFERENCES

Cohen, J., & Cohen, P. (1983). *Applied multiple regression/correlation analysis for the behavioral sciences* (2nd ed.). Hillsdale, NJ: Erlbaum.

Cook, T. D., & Campbell, D. T. (1979). *Quasi-experimentation: Design and analysis issues for field settings.* Boston: Houghton-Mifflin.

Crano, W. D., & Brewer, M. B. (1973). *Principles of research in social psychology.* New York: McGraw-Hill.

Reis, H. T., & Gable, S. L. (in press). Event-sampling and other methods for studying daily experience. In H. T. Reis & C. M. Judd (Eds.), *Handbook of research methods in social psychology.* New York: Cambridge University Press.

Reis, H. T., & Stiller, J. (1992). Publication trends in *JPSP:* A three decade review. *Personality and Social Psychology Bulletin, 18,* 465–472.

Sternberg, R. J., & Gordeeva, T. (1996). What makes an article influential? *Psychological Science, 7,* 69–75.

Wegener, D. T., & Fabrigar, L. R. (in press). Analysis and design for nonexperimentl data: Addressing causal and noncausal hypotheses. In H. T. Reis & C. M. Judd (Eds.), *Handbook of research methods in social psychology.* New York: Cambridge University Press.

West, S. G., Biesanz, J. C., & Pitts, S. C. (in press). Causal inference and generalization in field settings: Experimental and quasi-experimental designs. In H. T. Reis & C. M. Judd (Eds.), *Handbook of research methods in social psychology.* New York: Cambridge University Press.

Chapter 7

Doing Data Analyses and Writing Up Their Results

Selected Tricks and Artifices

ELENA L. GRIGORENKO

Every trade has its tricks, solutions to its own specific problems, and distinctive ways of doing something with which laypeople have a lot of trouble. The trade of data analysis (defined here as conceptualization, implementation, and presentation of data analyses), no less than cooking or painting, has tricks developed and preserved by generations of professional researchers to address peculiar issues, questions, and concerns. These tricks are of different natures. Some of them are simple rules of thumb extrapolated from experience (e.g., in presenting your results, do not forget to specify degrees of freedom for your analyses). Others are the result of scientific analysis (e.g., Becker, 1998). Some of these tricks are learned from formal sources (e.g., Abelson, 1995). Others are acquired through hanging around "experts" in the field and learning to use them, the way apprentices learn craft skills by watching the master.

Knowing tricks of the trade constitutes an informed way of carrying out data analysis. Correspondingly, a lack of this knowledge leads, on many occasions, to poor data analyses. Some researchers (Sutton & Maynard, 1993) have stated that poor data analysis amounts to faking (defined in the Oxford Dictionary as "contriving with poor material").

CLARIFICATIONS

The data world is huge. Moreover, the sheer quantity of data and summaries of data derived directly from or about individuals, groups, and cultures has increased rapidly in recent years and will increase more. These data stem from ability and achievement testing, measures of attitudes, surveys of satisfaction, socioeconomic indexes, and many other sources. These data constitute the basis for major economic, political, cultural, and educational decisions. In this ocean of data, the little sea of psychological data published in professional journals is almost negligible. Yet, there are certain ways these psychological data need to be handled.

The tricks and artifices that make up the content of this chapter are not designed to provide conceptual receptacles into which the sea of psychological data have to be poured. Moreover, they are not claimed to cover everything one needs to know about data analysis and result presentation. These tricks, rather, are "helpers" that may be thought of as being instrumental in interpreting and making general sense of data. Tricks are specific operations that show ways around some common difficulty – ways of avoiding a persistent problem (Becker, 1998). Before I present some of such tricks, consider three clarifications.

Clarification 1: Research Paradigms

Psychological data are collected within different research paradigms. Among the many classifications of research paradigms, consider the following one offered by Hammersley (1995).

First, *basic research* (also known as "blue skies" research) signifies experimental or theoretical work on understanding a context, population, foundation, or phenomenon with no particular use in view. Second, *strategic research* is viewed as research with a potential for application, but currently without any specification of what this application might be. Third, *applied research* is undertaken with a particular practical aim or objective in mind. These distinctions were made not to signify which research paradigm is best, but to recognize these paradigms' similarities and dissimilarities and respective contributions. Each of these paradigms has its own bag of data-analytic tricks. In this chapter, only those tricks that are shared by and useful for all three paradigms are considered.

Clarification 2: Quantitative and Qualitative Research

Traditionally, quantitative social science has been closely associated with positivism, assuming the primacy of the observable, the use

of knowledge for prediction and control, the analyzability of psychological data by quantitative methods, and the specific and important
role of statistical data analyses in conducting and summarizing psychological research. The role and significance of quantitative
research in psychology is linked to a nineteenth-century argument
over whether social science research should be carried out similarly
to that in physical sciences. This position was favored by a group of
philosophers (e.g., Mill, Durkheim, and others). The essence of the
positivistic point of view was (a) to regard social phenomena as facts
and things capable of investigation in an object-like manner; (b) to
view the social scientist as an observer of an independently existing
reality; and (c) to confine the social scientist to a position of neutral-
ity free of all bias, emotion, values, or anything that might compromise the objectivity of the research.

The development of positivism in the nineteenth century was
counterbalanced by the movement of idealism (e.g., Dilthey and
Weber). Idealistic philosophers challenged positivism by stating that
(a) the objects of social science cannot be separated from the thought
and mind of the investigator; (b) the relationship between the social
scientist and that which is being studied is not one of subject – object,
but of subject – subject; and (c) the social scientist inevitably influences the inquiry because he or she and the investigated phenomenon
are interactively linked through and by his or her values. In present-
day social science research the idealistic paradigm is represented by
constructivism, interpretivism, and hermeneutics (Guba & Lincoln,
1989; Schwandt, 1994; Woods, 1992), which, although different in
details, share the major assumptions of classic idealism.

The traces of this philosophical distinction between positivism
and idealism can be easily seen in different research methodologies. The positivistic stress on causality and prediction tends to
result in a more quantitative approach, whereas the idealistic call
for description and interpretation leads to a more qualitative
approach (Sciarra, 1999).

Positivism is now more often regarded as crude and misguided
(Reid, 1987). The view that the Cartesian assumption of a value-
free, presupposition-free, objective science does not hold has been
gaining in popularity. Yet, in terms of the day-to-day operation of
the machinery of psychological science (carried out primarily by

educational institutions, journal editorial boards, and granting foundations), the dominance of positivism, enumeration, and quantification is unquestionable. Nevertheless, "other" (descriptive/interpretive) types of analyses are slowly entering professional psychological circles. For example, of 249 clinical psychology dissertation abstracts published in 1965, only 2 (or 0.8%) used other than quantitative methods of data analyses (Keeley, Shemberg, & Zaynor, 1988). In 1992, of the 181 new counseling psychology PhD(s) surveyed, 15% of respondents used qualitative methods (Kopala, Suzuki, Goldman, & Galdi, 1997).

In this chapter, the distinction is made between quantitative (statistical) research and positivistic social science. Here statistical research does not imply a belief in purely positivistic methodology, but rather a belief in the usefulness of statistics when attempting to order and comprehend the complexities of substantial bodies of data. Since the late sixteenth and seventeenth centuries, the position stating that researchers' ideas about objectivity and factual accuracy are historical products rather than eternal principles of analysis (Young, 1979) has been gaining more popularity. Moreover, a datum itself is viewed as having evaluative implications and comprising non-neutral information for or against a particular point of view (Krige, 1979). Correspondingly, although qualitative and quantitative perspectives represent distinct methodological approaches and have differentiating characteristics, their merging is both possible and desirable (e.g., Ponterotto & Grieger, 1999). Many handbooks and textbooks have been written delineating specific tricks of quantitative and qualitative methodologies. Most of the tricks presented in this chapter are tricks arguably shared by or applicable to both methodological traditions. However, in keeping with the unbalanced situation in the field (where the Goddess of Enumeration rules almost exclusively), the chapter has some tricks specific only to quantitative analyses.

Clarification 3: The Chapter's "Yes(es)" and "No(s)"

Finally, it is necessary to define the limits of this chapter. This is done through what the chapter will do and what the chapter will not do.

The Chapter's "Yes(es)". This chapter presents some tricks of learning new things without obtaining new data, of doing data analy-

ses, and of making general sense of data. Thus, with the exception of
the details concerning the presentation of results discussed in the
Automatized Decorum section, the tricks presented here are more or
less logical. This does not assume that these tricks are based on or
require any knowledge of formal logic. These tricks allow one to get
into a certain mind-set, to see how to maximize the efficiency, accuracy, and adequacy of data analysis and presentation of results. These
tricks are thinking tricks, but the results of this thinking are clues to
where to look next, how to do data analyses, and how to present
research findings.

The Chapter's "No(s)". These tricks are not a set of instructions
on how to build models, how to do statistical analyses, or how to
select specific methods of analyses. If one wants to be instructed on
these issues, consider reviewing a collection of wonderful books dedicated to these purposes (both classics – e.g., Cohen & Cohen, 1983,
Tabachnik & Fidell, 1989, – and new – e.g., Joyce, 1999; Pentland,
Harvey, Lawton, & McColl, 1999).

THE PLACE OF DATA ANALYSIS

Everything has to be someplace. In publications, the data
analysis/results section follows background literature, hypothesis formulation, and description of methods but precedes discussion of the
results. In essence, this section makes possible the dialogue between
the accumulated data and newly acquired evidence.

On a broader scale of knowledge flow from the social sciences into
cultures, the stage of data analysis also plays a crucial role. In their
information cycle, for example, Bradley and Schaefer (1999) distinguish the following steps: (a) identifying a need for information; (b)
formulating a precise question; (c) selecting a measurement technique; (d) collecting data; (e) engaging in exploratory data analysis;
(f) formulating hypotheses, models, or both; (g) testing hypotheses;
(h) promulgating and critiquing results; (i) making decisions and/or
formulating policy based on results; and (j) returning to (a).

In addition to literally being "in the middle of action" both in any
single publication and in a broadly defined information cycle, and,
thus, linking old and new knowledge, data analyses have social signif-

icance. Consider, for example, the following words of Karl Pearson (as quoted in Smith, 1996, p. 380):

Florence Nightingale believed—and in all the actions of her life acted upon that belief—that the administrator could only be successful if he were guided by statistical knowledge. The legislator—to say nothing of the politician—too often failed for want of this knowledge. Nay, she went further: she held that the universe—including human communities—was evolved in accordance with a divine plan. . . . But to understand God's thoughts, she held we must study statistics, for these are the measure of his purpose. Thus the study of statistics was for her a religious duty.

Thus, the step of data analyses, both within a single study and within a broader defined information circle, has a tremendous importance. And like any important cultural tradition (whether a religious duty or not), data analyses and presentation of results have their regulations. Some of these regulations are considered in the next section.

NORMS OF DATA ANALYSIS

In studies of art, there are norms (standards/criteria) for evaluating the beauty of art. In the discipline of logic, there are norms of valid inferences. In schools of painting, there are norms of colors and techniques. In data analysis, there are also norms. One might argue that the very purpose of analyzing the data and, consequently, of presenting the results of these analyses, is the summary of an "objective" picture; therefore, introducing norms into data analyses will destroy objectivity. According to the position presented in this chapter, this argument is mistaken. Consider a typical range of definitions of the word "norm": an authoritative rule or standard; a principle of right action binding upon the members of a group and serving to guide, control, or regulate proper and acceptable behavior; a set standard of development or achievement usually derived from the average or median achievement of a large group (Merriam-Webster, 1969). Surely, there are principles of carrying out right actions binding upon the professional circle of data analysts and serving to guide, control, and regulate proper and acceptable behavior in those members of psychological community who wish to publish their work in professional journals.

Bradley and Schaefer (1999) distinguish two classes of normative principles of data analyses: intrinsic (methodological) and extrinsic (contextual). Intrinsic principles include such characteristics as simplicity, testability, consistency, lack of bias (unbiasedness), elegance, brevity, and fruitfulness. Extrinsic norms have been called "prima facie duties" (McCloskey, 1969); they include honesty, truthfulness, justice, compassion, and respect for opponents.

AXIOMS OF DATA ANALYSIS

Data analysis is driven by four major axioms, which, when paired, exhibit, at first glance, pairwise contradictions. Axioms 1 and 2 deal with the issue of subjectivity versus objectivity in data analysis; axioms 3 and 4 deal with the issue of data/presentation reduction versus completeness.

1. There are no "pure," "unbiased" analyses; any analysis requires an act of selection, an act of decision making and, therefore, an act of the formulation of a point of view. Any analysis is, rephrasing Thomas Kuhn's words, "theory laden." So, reading about and designing data analysis, we expect to see (from each other and ourselves) interpretations and assumptions.

2. Any data analysis should be carried out with the assumption that nothing that can be imagined is impossible – we should incorporate the possibility of the existence of the impossible in our analysis.

Let us break, for a moment, at this juncture and consider axioms 1 and 2 as a system. How come the first rule says that there is no unbiased, theory-free analysis, but the second rule states that all analyses should have some space for revealing the impossible? To appreciate these axioms in their unity, consider the following example (based on Sacks, 1987). In this example, a neurologist described his first and unexpected encounter with Tourette's syndrome (the neurological disorder that, among other things such as involuntary tics, makes people burst into loud and uncontrollable swearing) in a patient who came to his clinic. The neurologist was thrilled to see such a rare condition represented in his practice (the prevalence of Tourette's syndrome is <1%); on the way home, however, he saw two or three more cases whom he then unmistakably recognized as Touretters. The neurologist concluded that Tourette's syndrome cases had been there all along; he, however, had not been prepared to see them. The rule is that any data analysis should be shaped and designed from a well-defined and informed point of view (the neurologist was rightly surprised to see a patient with a condition of such a low prevalence). However, we should never assume that anything is impossible, that the impossible simply could not happen (the probability of the neurologist encountering three Touretters in one day is very low – $10^{-3} \times 10^{-3} \times 10^{-3}$ – but it did happen!)

3. Any coherent data analysis requires data reduction. Nobody wants a lot of (or all of) the details. John Tukey, a famous social sciences statistician, remarked that most tables contain far more information than anyone wants or needs, that mostly what we want to do is compare two numbers and see if they are the same or if one is bigger than the other; the rest of the numbers in all those cells are just noise, drowning out the message we are looking for (as quoted in Becker, 1998).

4. Any data analysis requires a full and coherent presentation. The description should have as much (or all) detail as necessary for anyone to reconstruct the analysis were the data available to him or her and were they to attempt a replication.

Similar to the relationship between axioms 1 and 2, the relationships between axioms 3 and 4 are rather "tense." How can one find the right balance between simplicity and completeness of data presentation? The skill of data analysis and data presentation is about meeting the requirements of the four axioms by maintaining the balance. The tricks listed below may be considered instrumental in achieving this balance.

A HANDFUL OF TRICKS

The tricks presented below are based on the assumption that difficulties encountered by students of data analyses and data presentation lie not so much with computational mechanics as with a larger perspective on what they are doing. These tricks may be thought of as aids in connecting the island of statistical analyses to the continent of psychological research, in linking the common sense of social scientists and the reality of enumeration. These tricks are treasures discovered through experience both published (Abelson, 1995; Becker, 1998; Bradley & Schaefer, 1999) and unpublished.

Automatized Decorum

The "stylish" presentation of results is characterized by a certain decorum. For experienced researchers the proprieties of data analyses I am about to discuss are automatized. Like washing hands before a meal or refilling an empty wine glass of a guest, automatized acts are done with little or no thought. Below I list selected characteristics of data analyses and result presentation decorum that become automatized with years of experience and a number of publications in peer-reviewed journals.

Report on What You Did to "Clean Up Your Act." The nature of social science data is such that often our data sets are characterized by all kinds of strangeness. Missing data, univariate and multivariate outliers, non-normality, heteroscedasticity, multicollinearity, and many other annoyances are rather common attributes of psychological data. The trick in dealing with these normally observed "abnormalities" is to screen for them, fight them, and report on the ways you managed to conquer them. Careful consideration of all these abnormalities is time consuming and no fun; however, dealing with them is a must for unbiased and honest data analyses. So, before you enter the wonderful, exciting world of data analysis, roll up your sleeves and do the dirty work of data screening.

Ratio of Cases to Variables. Virtually every statistical technique has a rule pertaining to the ratio of cases to variables. These rules are either listed in books on applied statistics (e.g., Tabachnik & Fidell, 1989) or passed on by word of mouth from more senior to more junior colleagues. The trick here is simple: Before deciding which statistical technique to apply, make sure that you have enough cases. For example, the golden rule of regression analyses assumes that you have 20 or more cases per each variable-predictor (i.e., per each variable appearing on the right-hand side of your equation). A bare minimum requirement for exploratory factor analyses is to have at least 10 times more cases than variables – for example, at least 200 cases for a 20-item survey the factor structure of which you investigate.

Tell Us Where You Hid the Bodies. Most psychological studies have to deal with a problem of missing data points. There are very few researchers out there who have been so fortunate as to work with complete data sets. Most of us have to use various tricks to fill in empty cells. The assortment of techniques is quite rich; feel free to choose one of the many, but, please do not forget to mention what you did and explain your choice (i.e., tell your audience why you picked a particular strategy to deal with missing data).

Do Not Make a Secret Out of Your Sample Size. The single most important driving force that makes people become scientists is curiosity. Curiosity is in researchers' veins. So, if you do not specify sample sizes for your analyses, your readers will ask you about them (not because they want to verify the power of your results, but because they are curious). Therefore, even though you provided a complete description of your sample size in the Method section, make sure that you present degrees of freedom for every single analysis you carried out.

Be Polite: Introduce Your Data First. A good introduction is usually followed by a nice time together. Make your reader comfortable – introduce your data in detail. The best way to do this is to present tables with a few descriptive statistics (usually, means and standard deviations; sometimes, higher-order moments of variable distributions) and simple correlations. Do not blow your reader away with heavy data analyses presented in the first paragraph of your Results section. Start with descriptives and bivariates and gradually work your way up to complex data analyses.

If You Do Not Have a Strong Opinion about Either, Do Both. These days there are many issues that provoke heated discussions among data analysts: hypothesis testing versus confidence intervals and effect sizes, stepwise approaches versus hierarchical approaches, exploratory analyses versus confirmatory analyses, principal components versus principal axes, correction for multiple comparisons versus implementation of multivariate techniques, to name a few. It is always better to have an opinion regarding these unresolved issues; then you can simply present your position in a sentence and leave any judging up to reviewers. If you do not have an opinion that you are ready to defend, present both sides of the issue, one in the main text, and one as a footnote.

Finding the Major Premise

Any data analysis and result presentation should be based on the main argument. What is it we are trying to show? To understand the power of this trick, consider a classical logical argument: *All men are mortal; Socrates was a man; therefore Socrates was a mortal.* The standard logical analysis separates three components of this argument: *a major premise* (a statement of a general truth already known – all men are mortal), a *minor premise* (a statement of a particular fact also agreed to – Socrates was a man); and a *conclusion* (a derivation that is possible under the assumption that the minor premise is a special case of, and therefore included in, the major premise).

Judith Harris (1995) shook up the psychological community when she stated the major premise of her research, namely, that, when it comes down to adolescence, family influences do not matter. It is typical of the psychological community to react with uproar to statements contradicting the community's accepted point of view. The problem, however, is that this statement is not only counter to the sacred grounds of developmental psychology – Harris's arguments come from two different claims that do not jibe with one another. Her argument was supported by two conclusions she arrived at based on her review of the literature: (a) adolescents are not trying to be (and they are not) like adults and (b) adolescents are trying to be like their peers (like other adolescents). Therefore, she said, whatever our parents do to us is overshadowed, in the long run, by what our peers do to us. Let us try to reconstruct from these conclusions the underlying logical arguments.

Harris's first conclusion is that adolescents are not trying to be like adults (or, reformulated for simplicity, adolescents do not behave like adults). Harris's second conclusion is that adolescents are trying to be like their peers (or, reformulated once again, adolescents behave like their peers). As for the minor premise, it should either generalize to the subject or to the discussed characteristic. Thus, there are two possible alternatives:

- Adolescents do not behave like adults → adults behave like adults → adolescents are not adults.
- Adolescents behave like their peers → peers behave as peers → adolescents are peers.

Each of the two conclusions comes from an independent claim. But how can one find a bridge between them? From the standpoint of formal logic they cannot be linked.

What makes an argument, stated in incomplete form, compelling and unanswerable? According to Becker (1998), it is that major premises are often tightly linked to people's everyday experiences, and, therefore, do not require demonstration of their logical roots (i.e., the structure of the argument). Thus, an often dismissed part of the analysis is rather *psycho*logical than logical – we need to reveal a pattern in daily life producing a feeling of familiarity, a kind of commonsense certainty that makes incomplete arguments fly.

The analytical trick here is to identify known facts as parts of an incomplete logical argument. What is quite often seen in papers is that a researcher states a conclusion and supports it with a statement of fact that serves as the minor premise of a syllogism that is never openly and fully stated. The attempt to unfold the argument and deliver it to the audience is worth a lot. This trick allows us to extract the hidden major premise and to try to reconstruct the link between the conclusion and the premises. An incomplete logical argument is what usually provokes confusion and suspicion in research communities. The trick is to *state* the logical argument underlying the data analysis and result presentation.

The "How to Generate Exceedingly Wise Thoughts" Trick

This trick was first patented by Raggedy Ann, who, according to witnesses' accounts (Gruelle, 1993), generated great thoughts every time her head got stuffed with clean white cotton. The trick has to do with explaining implausible relationships – relationships revealed by your data but contradictory to a body of the literature and, often, to common sense. This trick has many subtricks. In particular,

- Never assume that the phenomenon you study stays the same. In psychological reality, nothing stays the same and nothing is the same as anything else. Psychological phenomena are historically

contingent, culturally sensitized, geographically influenced combinations of a variety of processes. The bottom line is never to
ignore a problem of interest to you because it has already been
studied by someone else. Avoid the fallacy of the type "Why
bother? Such-and-such just published a paper on this . . ." Think
of clean white cotton put in Raggedy's head – the head is the same,
but the thoughts are wiser.

- Do not think *variables*, think *sets of variables*. For example, the eva-
siveness of the finding linking single-parent families to delinquency
is, in part, explainable by this fallacy – the finding is very robust for
single-parent families living in troubled neighborhoods (i.e., not
one, but many variables matter).

- Exercise proper skepticism even regarding your own data. Look for
other opinions; always ask your colleagues to read your paper
before submitting it to a journal.

- Do not be afraid of "unexpected" findings. When you encounter
one, try to change the focus of the analysis (Bollen & Phillips,
1982), keeping in mind the conceptual protection of the artifact
(Abelson, 1995). For example, William Caruso, the guru of the
ethnography of early childhood, discovered the importance of protection from distraction for preschool children's play by attempting
to study "antisocial" play-related behaviors of otherwise sociable
children.

In short, the Raggedy trick is about learning how to question, how
not to accept blindly the beliefs of our senior colleagues and our own
beliefs.

The Machine Trick

The Machine Trick represents one of the best mental tools for
thinking through the model-building step of data analysis.
Whatever kind of multivariate modeling is to be used in your analyses, to mentally prove the plausibility of your model, consider the
following trick:

Design the machine that will produce the result your analysis indicates
occurs routinely in the situation you have studied. Make sure the machine
has all of the necessary parts (engine, gears, belts, buttons, and so on), everything that is necessary to get the desired result. Strangely enough, psychologists usually study situations that are rather undesirable (e.g., alcohol abuse),

and thus, the machine product will not, in fact, be desirable. This "undesirability of the outcome," however, should not stop us from proceeding with our mental experiment.

In order to see the machine in action, consider a phenomenon you do not like, for example, your subjects not showing up for your experiments. The next step is to assume that this, in fact, is the wanted rather than the unwanted result: It is meant to be that your subjects sign up but do not show up for your experiments. Let us assume that Tolkien's Morgoth, the first Dark Lord, organized an elaborate machine that produces exactly the result you have. You would love to understand how this machine works, but Morgoth does not respond to your inquiries, so you need to apply the technology of "reverse engineering" and reproduce the mechanism from the product.

Imagining such a machine gives us a chance to consider including in our equations the variables that we otherwise would have left out, driven, possibly, by our professional values, biases, and attitudes. The rule is that the machine will not work unless it has everything it needs to get the job done, to consider everything that might contribute to the occurrence of the phenomenon. The Machine Trick is especially helpful in dealing with the phenomenon of Occam's razor, which is the occurrence of focusing on aspects of events (phenomena, variables) judged to be essential and ignoring other aspects, the occurrence of an intentional separation of observations from context.

Establishing Causes

Psychologists like to think by using causal language and saying that something "causes" something else. The issue of cause versus consequence has a long-standing tradition in philosophy, the main argument being that, on many occasions, cause is difficult to separate from chance and from the simple fact of sequence. About 99% of psychologists using causal language do not bother to engage in philosophical arguments. They simply use classical pragmatic methods in establishing the rules of causality. In the world of data analyses, we cannot get anything done without these rules, and yet they have serious flaws in their supporting logic, they are vulnerable to attack, and they have been shown to be less and do less than is expected of them.

The main rule of establishing causality is explicitly pronounced in the language of variables. The analyst identifies a "dependent variable" (something that varies along some dimension) and an "independent variable" (something whose variation causes variation in the dependent variable). Thus, if the measure of the dependent variable changes in some regular way when the measure of the independent variable changes, the relationship is assumed to be causal (Ragin, 1987).

This line of logic, however, is not flawless. These days, any course of introduction to statistics makes its students learn that correlation is not causation. But how, for example, can we figure out to what extent parental social position, education, occupation, and income affect (and thus cause) people's IQ?

A traditional family of procedures is based on implementing quasi-experimental factoring out of the relative influence of the several causes we think of as explaining or accounting for the outcome we are interested in studying (e.g., IQ). These procedures include various stepwise and hierarchical analyses. These analyses have been criticized multiple times, the main argument being that the notion of estimating the influence of a variable by holding other factors constant is untenable because of the nonrandom distribution of the variables introduced in such a way (the so-called selection problem; Lieberson, 1985). There are four major assumptions underlying this family of methods (Becker, 1998). The first underlying assumption of this approach is that all the causes involved in the production of an effect operate more or less simultaneously and continuously. Moreover, these procedures require an assumption that the variables proposed as causes operate independently, that is, that each makes its own contribution to the variation in the dependent variable. Third, even when interaction effects of independent variables are considered, the interactions themselves are treated as if they contribute to the variation in the dependent variable simultaneously and continuously. The final assumption made here is that all causes are additive.

In reality, variables have temporal order and occur in a recognizable sequence. Causes often exist in a kind of symbiotic relationship; there are also some antagonistic relationships between causes. The logic of techniques described above does not provide any special way of dealing either with the time or the interaction factors; the trick is not to buy into the visual surface of path diagrams purporting to deal with temporal sequences but in reality being only visual metaphors for them. The trick here is to be careful in nominating some variables as causal. Fully algorithmic approaches to establishing causality are never going to work. Consider, for example, the argument of Supples (1970, pp. 90–91):

> In recent years, mechanisms whose properties are not fully characterized are referred to as black boxes, especially in communication and information science. Back of this concept of a black box is a fundamental message about causal mechanisms which represents perhaps the most important philosophical separation between the classical tradition of Aristotle, Descartes, and Kant on the one hand, and the modern temperament on the other. . . . The analysis of causes and their identification must always be relative to a conceptual framework, and there is no successful line of argument apparently that can show that a particular conceptual framework represents some ultimate and correct view about the structure of the world. From the standpoint of either scientific investigation or philosophical analysis it can fairly be said that one man's mechanism is another man's black box. I mean by this that the mechanisms postulated and used by one generation are mechanisms that are to be explained and understood themselves in terms of more primitive mechanisms by the next generation.

The bottom line is that there is no inference of causality without an interpretation. Empirical and methodological techniques involving the notions of conditional probability and partitioned variance might be helpful in identifying causal variables, but often create the illusion of the resolution of the causality problem without actually resolving it.

The Wittgenstein Trick

This trick is referred to as the Wittgenstein trick because it was provoked by a passage in Wittgenstein's *Philosophical Investigations* (1973, §621):

> Let us not forget this: when I raise my arm, my arm goes up. And the problem arises: what is left over if I subtract the fact that my arm goes up from the fact that I raise my arm?

This is the essence of the trick. In conducting data analyses, always ask yourself a question: If I take away from an event, phenomenon, or object X some quality Y, what is left? Think of the answer not in terms of the percentage of variance but in terms of the psychological meaning of the residual. The intent of this trick is to help us separate what is central to our understanding of a phenomenon from the particular example in which it is embedded.

How Much Detail?

One of the most powerful tricks of data analysis and presentation of results is finding the balance between what you, as an author, know and what you would like your reader to know. There is a lot to be said for the art of losing information for the sake of gaining understanding. Nothing is so important in presenting the results of data analysis as the attempt to arrive at helpful simplification. Any psychological phenomenon is embedded in or related to many events, facts, relationships, and actions. In presenting the data, one must have a model or a conceptual framework. In delivering facts, one must descend from the abstract to the concrete, from the model to the data. The crucial moment here is to detect the most informative abstraction, to leave out the unimportant in order to make the important more transparent.

The Replicability Trick

Social events, such as particular economic conditions or historical circumstances, never can be replicated. We cannot say, "Let us rerun the Great Russian Revolution and see what happens." The same is applicable to most psychological phenomena: human intentionality inevitably introduces nonreplicability. But do we really have an excuse for buying into this logic?

Our savior here is the replicability trick, which establishes the correspondence between the generality of a finding and the degree of its replicability (Abelson, 1995). The narrower the generality of the finding, the more stringent the demands for its replicability; the more local and constrained the findings are, the more likely the original claim is to be supported.

Thus, replications can be divided into a number of categories. First, exact replications refer to the strategy of reconstructing the study in its nearly identical form. It is hard to believe, but the research literature is rather well populated with reports of failures of exact replications. That is why, partially, many professional journals expect their submitters to report at least two, preferably more, linked studies in one publication; this, if it does not address the problem of replicability of results, at least creates the illusion of such. Second, a family of modest replications refers to a tradition of modifying one or two experimental parameters (e.g., modifying treatment or response indicators). Third, and the most widely spread type of replications, are distant replications, whereby researchers replicate some major finding (e.g., anxiety influences work productivity) but specific characteristics of the design, and, often, settings of the study, vary dramatically.

So, the trick here is to anticipate the degree of replicability of your results. This knowledge is extremely important for you as an experimenter (and we should be able to be honest with ourselves). Moreover, in writing up your results, it is important to spell out all the limitations of your study that might prevent your findings from being replicated.

The Trick of Verification

The trick of verification is another that allows us to make the most of the collected data. The trick here is to go beyond the obvious, to challenge our own assumptions. As an illustration of the necessity for this trick, consider one of the most well-known stories told by Herodotus in *History of Ancient Greece* (1814):

King Croesus was deeply concerned about the growing power of the Persians. He considered starting a war and sought advice from his oracles. Of many, Croesus decided to pick only one oracle to trust. To select the trustworthy oracle, he sent messengers with the instruction that they were to approach each oracle on precisely the 100th day after being sent and simply to ask them what Croesus was doing that day. On the selected day, Croesus chopped up a tortoise and some lamb's meat and boiled them together in a bronze cauldron with a bronze lid on it. Many different answers were given to Croesus' messengers; all were wrong. But the priestesses of Delphi said, "A smell steals over my senses, the smell of a hard-shelled tortoise, seethed in bronze with the meat of lambs, mingled together; bronze is the base beneath, and bronze the vestment upon it." When the Delphi oracles' response was delivered to Croesus, he decided that they were the only true oracles. Croesus thanked Apollo, the god of Delphi, with enormous quantities of gold and silver, sacrificed animals, and other gifts and sent the messenger back to Delphi. The question this time, however, was different. Croesus wanted to know whether he should make war upon the Persians. The priestesses answered that the war upon the Persians would destroy a mighty empire. Croesus was inspired by this answer. What he did not apprehend, however, was that the empire referred to was his own. (Rawlinson, 1932)

A view of truth as statements that correspond to reality is helpful but by itself is insufficient for understanding the underlying phenomenon. A helpful trick in verifying a conclusion is to consider alternatives.

Bonus Points

The simplest trick of all is to try to collect from your review panel (consisting of either journal reviewers or dissertation committee members) as many bonus points as possible. There are a number of characteristics of one's data analysis and presentation of results that earn positive comments from reviewers. These are no-lose targets.

> *Simplicity.* Given two (or more) possible expressions of the same idea, the simpler is usually preferable. The reason is a simple one: a simple idea lends itself more effectively to analysis.
>
> *Generality.* Generality assumes that form can be separated from content without essential loss of meaning.
>
> *Applicability.* Applicability assumes the presence of links between research and reality. The use of data and models has become extremely pervasive in scientific culture; mathematical results have a high credibility, but the main validity criterion is in the question of where and how the results of the study can be applied in the larger world.
>
> *Clarity.* In order to abstract the messages from data and make use of them, reports should be clearly and simply written and presented. It is important not to be wordy, but it is also important not to be short of words. The nature of psychological research is such that often many studied phenomena are represented more effectively in words than in numbers. Consider, for example, *The Diary of Anne Frank.* What amount of data could be compared to this small book communicating the meaning of the Nazi era so effectively?

DATA ANALYSIS AS PRINCIPLED ARGUMENT: THE ABELSONIAN VIEW

Last, but not least, there are several properties of data, its analysis, and presentation labeled by Bob Abelson (1995) by the acronym

MAGIC. The MAGIC stands for *magnitude, articulation, generality, interestingness,* and *credibility.*

The stronger the quantitative *magnitude* of support for the qualitative gain made by the researcher, the more convincing the result. The larger the size of effect captured in the analysis, the more solid, replicable, and susceptible to validation is the result of the study.

The higher the degree of *articulation* of the results and conclusions, and of the degree of comprehensible detail of the analysis, the higher the degree of professionalism demonstrated by the researcher. For Abelson, it is not enough to present mean differences – they ought to be explained.

The conclusions obtained from data analysis can be described in terms of their *generality*. For Abelson, generality indicates the breadth of applicability of the conclusions. For the majority of psychological studies the associated circumstances are rather narrow.

The story told by the data should be theoretically *interesting*. Creating an acceptable scientific story, explaining the meaning of data, and making inferences beyond the data constrain the telling of the story: (a) the story must work, be coherent both internally and externally, and take us from the beginning to the end; (b) the story must be congruent with the facts; and (c) it has to have the potential to change people's beliefs about an important issue.

Finally, the believability of a research claim is determined by *credibility*. Credibility requires both methodological soundness and theoretical coherence. Statistical errors (whether odd data, a flawed selection of research design, or erroneous statistical procedures) tend to be easily noticed and criticized by those with an interest in results. Following Tukey (1969), Abelson states that the requisite skills for producing credible statistical narratives are not unlike those of a good detective. In essence, the task of the researcher is to solve an interesting case: the unique pattern of the data. In this peculiar investigation of the data, the researcher needs to rule out alternatives and confront skeptics who do not want to believe in the data.

TO CONCLUDE BUT NOT TO FINISH

The tricks of data analyses do not exist and cannot ever be mastered in isolation from conceiving, designing, implementing, and interpreting research. In fact, serious scientists repeatedly move back and forth among these aspects of research. A psychologist chooses the sample so that the ascertainment strategy reflects the conception of the research, but he or she will surely modify the conception on the basis of what the sample shows. And this modification of the general idea of the study will, no doubt, influence the interpretation of the results. And so forth. Social science research has never been and will never be represented as a neat, logical, clean-cut process (Becker, 1998). Clifford Geertz has provided us with a good description of the reality of social science research:

One works *ad hoc* and *ad interim*, piecing together thousand-year histories with three-week massacres, international conflicts with municipal ecologies. The economics of rice and olives, the politics of ethnicity and religion, the working of language or war, must, to some extent, be soldered into the final construction. So must geography, trade, art, and technology. The result, inevitably, is unsatisfactory, lumbering, shaky, and badly formed: a grand contraption. The anthropologist, or at least one who wishes to complicate his contraptions, not close them in upon themselves, is a manic tinkerer adrift with his wits. (Geertz, 1995, p. 20)

The tricks of data analyses are to be used in and out of order, wherever and whenever it looks like they might advance our understanding of psychological phenomena.

REFERENCES

Abelson, R. (1995). *Statistics as principled argument*. Hillsdale, NJ: Erlbaum.
Becker, H. S. (1998). *Tricks of the trade*. Chicago: The University of Chicago Press.
Bollen, K. A., & Phillips, D. P. (1982). Imitative suicides: A national study of the effects of television news stories. *American Sociological Review, 47*, 802–809.
Bradley, W. J., & Schaefer, K. C. (1999). *The uses and misuses of data and models*. Thousand Oaks, CA: Sage.
Cohen, J., & Cohen, P. (1983). *Applied multiple regression/correlation analysis for the behavioral sciences*. Hillsdale, NJ: Erlbaum.
Geertz, C. (1995). *After the fact: two countries, four decades, one anthropologist*. Cambridge, MA: Harvard University Press.
Grulle, J. (1993). *Raggedy Ann stories*. New York, NY: Simon & Schuster Books for Young Readers.
Guba, E. G., & Lincoln, Y. S. (1989). *Fourth-generation evaluation*. Newbury Park, CA: Sage.
Hammersley, M. (1995). *The politics of social research*. London: Sage.

Harris, J. R. (1995). Where is the child's environment? A group socialization theory of development. *Psychological Review, 102,* 458–489.

Herodotus (1814). Herodotus, translated from the Greek, with notes. Philadelphia, PA: E. Earle.

Joyce, J. (1999). *The foundations of causal decision theory.* New York: Cambridge.

Keeley, S. M., Shemberg, K. M., & Zaynor, L. (1988). Dissertation research in clinical psychology: Beyond positivism? *Professional Psychology: Research and Practice, 19,* 216–222.

Kopala, M., Suzuki, L. A., Goldman, L., & Galdi, L. (1987, August). *Dissertation research in counseling psychology: Topics, methods, and qualitative training.* Paper presented at the annual meeting of the American Psychological Association, Chicago.

Krige, J. (1979). What's so great about facts? In J. Irvine, I. Miles, & J. Evans (Eds.), *Demystifying social statistics* (pp. 53–62). London, England: Pluto Press.

Lieberson, S. (1985). *Making it count.* Berkley and Los Angeles: University of California Press.

McCloskey, H. J. (1969). *Meta-ethics and normative ethics.* The Hague, The Netherlands: Martinus Nijhoff.

Merriam-Webster, A. (1969). *Webster's seventh new collegiate dictionary.* Springfield, MA: G. & C Merriam Company.

Pentland, W. E., Harvey, A. S., Lawton, M. P., & McColl, M. A. (Eds.) (1999). *Time use research in the social sciences.* New York: Kluwer.

Ponterotto, J. G., & Grieger, I. (1999). Merging qualitative and quantitative perspectives in a research identity. In M. Kopala & L. A. Suzuki (Eds.), *Using qualitative methods in psychology* (pp. 49–62). Thousand Oaks, CA: Sage.

Ragin, C. (1987). *The comparative method: Moving beyond qualitative and quantitative strategies.* Berkeley: University of California Press.

Rawlinson, G. (1932). *The history of Herodotus.* New York: Tudor Publishing.

Reid, S. (1997). *Working with statistics.* Cambridge, England: Polity Press.Sacks, O. W. (1987). *The man who mistook his wife for a hat and other clinical tales.* New York: Simon and Schuster.

Schwandt, T. A. (1994). Constructivist, interpretivist approaches to human inquiry. In N. K. Denzin & Y. S. Lincoln (Eds.), *Handbook of qualitative research* (pp. 118–137). Thousand Oaks, CA: Sage.

Sciarra, D. (1999). The role of the qualitative researcher. In M. Kopala & L. A. Suzuki (Eds.), *Using qualitative methods in psychology* (pp. 37–48). Thousand Oaks, CA: Sage.

Smith, A. (1996). Mad cows and ecstasy: Chance and choice in an evidence-based society. *Journal of the Royal Statistical Society, 159,* 367–383.

Supples, P. (1970). *A probabilistic theory of causality.* Amsterdam: North-Holland Publishing.

Sutton, M., & Maynard, A. (1993). Are drug policies based on 'fake' statistics? *Addiction, 88,* 455–458.Tabachnik, B. G., & Fidell, L. S. (1989). *Using multivariate statistics.* New York: Harper & Row.

Tukey, J. W. (1969). Analyzing data: Sanctification or detective work? *American Psychologist, 24,* 83–91.

Wittgenstein, L. (1973). Philosophische Untersuchungen [Philosophical investigations; the English text of the third edition. Translated by G. E. M. Anscombe]. New York, NY: Macmillan.

Woods, P. (1992). Symbolic interactionism: Theory and method. In M. D. LeCompte, W. D., Millnoy, & J. Preissle (Eds.), *The handbook of qualitative research* (pp. 337–404). San Diego, CA: Academic Press.
Young, R. (1979). Why are figures so significant? The role and critique of quantification. In J. Irvine, I. Miles, & J. Evans (Eds.). *Demystifying social statistics* (pp. 63–74). London, England: Pluto Press.

Chapter 8

Results That Get Results

Telling a Good Story

PETER SALOVEY

any psychologists think the Results section is the driest part of any journal article, that the idea in this portion of the manuscript is simply to present the data and move on. For students reading journal articles as class assignments, the Results section is often the one skipped. It is considered boring at best, inscrutable at worst, and whatever one needs to know is summarized in the opening paragraphs of the Discussion anyway. It does not have to be this way, however. In this chapter, I argue that there are techniques for writing a Results section that at least make it readable, if not thrilling.

The key is to tell a good story. In recent years, the idea that mental representations are organized as stories is quite popular. Jefferson Singer and I argued that the self is a story – that who we are really is a set of stories that we tell about ourselves (Singer & Salovey, 1993). The editor of this volume, Robert Sternberg (1998), has described love as a story. Sternberg maintains that there are various kinds of romantic scripts guiding our conception of how relationships unfold. Robert Abelson (1995) described the way in which investigators make claims with statistical tests as a "principled argument," that is, a kind of story. Perhaps the boldest idea comes from one of the fathers of artificial intelligence, Roger Schank (1990), who claimed that all of cognition is, essentially, a story. Well, if the self, love, statistics, and all of cognition are organized as stories, certainly the idea that a Results section can be a story should not strike you as too radical an idea.

In the remainder of this chapter, I provide some rules to help you craft a Results section as a good story. These rules are not meant to be followed religiously or blindly, but more often than not they help to increase the readability of your manuscript. I believe strongly that every writer needs to find his or her own voice and style, and so rules like these are more like advice from a friendly aunt or uncle rather than laws passed by the state legislature. And, as my father says, "Advice is like a gift. Accept it graciously, but then do what you want with it after the gift-giver is gone." This chapter does not repeat valuable information that you can find in the *Publication Manual of the American Psychological Association* (APA, 1994) nor does it provide a primer on psychological statistics or the proper reporting of statistical tests. I am going to assume you already know all that and that you have a copy of the *Publication Manual* on your desk. Instead, the focus in this chapter is on the Results section as whole, and how to make this segment of your article as exciting as possible.

BEGIN WITH WHAT IS MOST IMPORTANT

The best organizational strategy for a manuscript reporting an experiment or set of experiments is usually not the order in which the investigator conducted the data analysis. Too often, Results sections have the feel of a data analysis archive – a listing of every statistical procedure to which the data were subjected in the order in which the investigator entered them into the computer. It is a much better strategy to dispense with preliminary analyses as quickly as possible and get to the central findings. Peripheral analyses can be reported later. The most effective articles first present findings indicating that the study was properly conducted – manipulation checks for an experiment, for example – but then move quickly to the main event.

Much of my current work explores how to maximize the persuasiveness of messages promoting a health behavior such as obtaining a mammogram or applying sunscreen. In a typical study, my team goes to a public beach and distributes different kinds of brochures. After sunbathers have read the brochures, a short questionnaire assessing attitudes toward sunscreen is handed out. Finally, coupons are dispensed that can be cashed in for actual bottles of sunscreen later in the day (e.g., Detweiler, Bedell, Salovey, Pronin, & Rothman, 1999).

The most important potential finding in a study like this one is if different brochures actually influenced whether sunbathers obtained a bottle of sunscreen. The impact of the brochures on attitudes is interesting too, but not nearly as important as whether we observed actual behavior change. As such, it is probably a better strategy in the Results section of an article reporting these findings to present the influence of the brochures on coupon redemption for sunscreen samples prior to the attitudinal data. The reader should not have to read the entire Results section to know whether – bottom line – the experiment worked. If the most important question is, "So, did different brochures encourage people actually to use sunscreen?", then the answer should be provided as early in the Results section as possible.

KEEP THE ORDER OF PRESENTATION PARALLEL TO OTHER SECTIONS OF THE ARTICLE

While we are on the topic of the order of presenting findings, it is also generally a good idea to try to keep the order of your Results section consistent with that of the Introduction and Method sections. So in the example above, if I plan to discuss the influence of different kinds of brochure content on actual sunscreen use before I discuss its influence on attitudes toward skin cancer and sun blocking products, my Introduction and Method sections should also present relevant material in the same order. In the Introduction, the literature describing sunscreen use should be presented before the literature on attitudes. My hypotheses about actual behavior should be delineated before the hypotheses concerning attitudes. Likewise, in the Method section, it would be preferable to describe the operationalization of sunscreen use (i.e., coupons redeemed) before the operationalization of relevant attitudes (i.e., seven-point Likert scales).

PROVIDE TOP-DOWN STRUCTURE

You have all read Results sections, I'm sure, in which the author simply lists finding after finding, in no apparent order, with no reference to the goals of the experiment or the conclusions that should be drawn. I know that I've read many such Results sections in, alas, the first drafts of doctoral dissertations. This style reflects a mistaken belief that somehow in the Results section, the investigator is just supposed to lay out the facts without editorial comment. Interpretation is saved for the Discussion. This approach leads to very dry Results sections and poorly integrated manuscripts.

A better approach when presenting each finding is to remind the reader why those data are proffered and then to reflect on the relationship between the reported data and the original hypotheses described, one hopes, in the Introduction. So, for example, let's imagine a journal article reporting a study of the effects of mood on the recall of childhood memories. In this experiment, happy or sad moods were induced in a group of participants, who then described the first memory about their childhood that came to mind. So, a participant watched either a pleasant or unpleasant film and was then asked to recall a childhood memory. Then, the participant rated the memory on various scales. At the end of the session, the participant completed a set of mood scales as a manipulation check to make sure that the moods induced by the films lasted for the entire experimental session.

Assume that we are writing the part of the Results section having to do with the manipulation check. Although it is certainly straightforward and clear to write "Participants assigned to the happy condition reported more positive moods ($M = 30.04$) than those assigned to the sad condition ($M = 10.04$), $F(1, 99) = 4.60$, $p < .05$," it is probably better to remind the reader *why* you are reporting these findings and *what* should be concluded on the basis of them:

In order to verify that the moods induced by the films lasted for the entire experimental session, participants completed a mood scale before leaving the laboratory. Participants who watched the pleasant film reported more positive moods ($M = 30.04$) than those who watched the unpleasant film ($M = 10.04$), $F(1, 99) = 4.60$, $p < .05$. These differences suggest that the moods were properly induced and that they were strong enough to be felt 20 minutes later.

Although this version is a bit longer, it reminds the reader why the data were collected, and it tells the reader what to conclude on the basis of these findings. As Daryl Bem, one of the best writers of journal articles in our field, says, "by announcing each result clearly in prose before wading into the numbers and statistics, and by summarizing frequently, you permit a reader to decide just how much detail he or she wants to pursue at each juncture and to skip ahead to the next main point whenever that seems desirable" (Bem, 1987, p. 185).

DON'T LET THE STRUCTURE OF THE STATISTICAL TEST DETERMINE THE STRUCTURE OF YOUR PROSE

A frequently used strategy for writing a Results section is to arrange the output from your favorite statistical software package (e.g., SAS, SPSS, BMDP) on your desk and then to write your prose while staring at these printouts. This approach can lead to sentences that bear more of a resemblance to the textbook from your Introduction to Analysis of Variance course than to an article that you actually hope someone might read. Once again, the theme of this chapter, "tell a story" is your guide. And the output of an ANOVA is rarely a good story.

Consider the following example of what I call *statistics-based prose:*

A two-way, 2 × 2 between-subjects ANOVA was performed on ratings of the vividness of childhood memories in which the independent variables were participant sex (male or female) and induced mood (happy or sad). There was no main effect for sex ($F(1, 99) = 0.20$, n.s.), but there was a main effect for mood ($F(1, 99) = 7.89$, $p < .01$) and a sex by mood interaction ($F(1, 99) = 12.30, p < .01$). Happy people had more vivid memories than sad people, overall. This effect was stronger for women than it was for men. As can be seen in the results from Tukey's studentized range test reported in Table 1, the vividness of happy and sad female participants' memories differed significantly, but the vividness of happy and sad male participants' memories did not.

Notice how in this passage we have no idea what was actually discovered until the very end, and we are still not really sure of the direction of the reported effects. By focusing on the terms in the ANOVA output, the author has communicated very little about what really went on in this experiment. There is also a tendency for statistics-based prose to be written in a passive voice.

Compare the previous passage to the following:

Table 1 provides the vividness ratings for men and women who experienced happy or sad moods. The childhood memories of men and women did not differ in vividness, $F(1, 99) = 0.20$, n.s. The most striking finding, however, was that the usual tendency for happy people to report more vivid memories than people in sad moods, $F(1, 99) = 7.89$, $p < .01$, was stronger for women than men, as indicated by a significant sex by mood interaction, $F(1, 99) = 12.30$, $p < .01$. This finding is consistent with the hypothesis that mood has a more pronounced effect on the quality of childhood memories among women than men and was confirmed with the Tukey's studentized range test reported in Table 1.

Notice how in this rewriting of the same passage, the story (not just the childhood memories of happy women) is more vivid. By side-stepping the language of analysis of variance (for the most part) and, instead, reporting what happened, the reader has a clearer sense of the empirical bottom line.

There are a few other things to note about the second passage. First, the author refers to a table where the cell means can be located. Perhaps even the ANOVA F-statistics and p-values could be moved to that table too, uncluttering the text further. Second, it is always good form to present descriptive statistics (e.g., cell means) before inferential statistics (F, t, chi-square, etc.). In other words, describe the findings – in terms with which the reader is familiar – before testing whether the trend is statistically significant or not. When presented the other way around, it is as if the author cares more about p-values meeting some criterion than the more general pattern in the data, and the Results section can convey the impression of a fishing expedition rather than hypothesis-driven science.

JUSTIFY THE SELECTION OF STATISTICAL PROCEDURES AND TESTS

Often it is obvious how best to analyze your data. In the example of the experiment concerning mood and childhood memory, it seems fairly obvious that cell means will be reported by mood condition and, perhaps, sex followed by some kind of analysis of variance. But sometimes one has a choice of which statistical methods to use, and it is often helpful to provide the reader with a brief justification for your selection.

Consider, once again, our work on how different kinds of persuasive brochures affect the use of sunscreen by beach-goers. Assume, for now, that we are comparing two kind of brochures, one that describes the benefits of sunscreen use and one that describes the costs of failing to use sunscreen (see Rothman & Salovey, 1997, for a discussion concerning which of these kinds of brochures should be more persuasive). To examine the differential influence of these brochures on participants' redemption of coupons for free bottles of sunscreen, we would likely report the percentage of participants who turned in coupons by brochure condition. But we could test the significance of the difference between these percentages in a number of ways, for example, using logistic regression, log-linear model fitting, or analysis of variance with arc-sine transformation. In selecting an approach, it is often helpful to tell the reader why you made the particular choice. For example:

Because sunscreen use was measured as a dichotomous, categorical variable and we wanted to determine the odds of coupon redemption among participants who read the first brochure as compared to those who read the second brochure, we analyzed the data using logistic regression.

Investigators often reduce the number of dependent variables under consideration using principal components or factor analysis. Once again, it is helpful to indicate to readers why a particular method was selected, such as principal axis or maximum likelihood, and why the factors were left unrotated or rotated according to some criterion, like varimax or promax. What assumptions were made about the data that justified the factor extraction method and rotation? Often investigators seem to select such methods by default – such as a varimax rotation – without much forethought. Similarly, the investigator should rationalize how he or she selected a certain number of factors to describe. Often "eigenvalues greater than one" is used as the criterion when other standards, such as interpretability or an elbow in a scree plot, may be more sensible.

The point is that the selection of statistical procedures should be guided by the assumptions the investigator is making about the data, and these assumptions should be made explicit to readers. Too often, the default procedures in statistical packages drive the tests reported.

Early in a good Results section (and sometimes at various transition points later on), the author furnishes for the reader a description of the general approach to analyzing the data, assumptions made along the way, citations to nonstandard procedures, and justification for the selection of procedures from among an array of options.

THOROUGH REPORTING IS GOOD FORM

Earlier, I discussed why it is good practice to provide readers with a description of what was discovered (e.g., cell means) before turning to inferential statistics, such as analyses of variance. There are similar rules of thumb that apply to other statistical procedures. I would not characterize these as hard-and-fast rules – there are many times when it is reasonable to make exceptions – but in general it is good practice to follow them.

For one, when analyses are sensitive to the correlations among your variables, a table of these correlations should be provided. For example, often investigators report multiple regression analyses in which the influence of a set of "predictors" on a "criterion" is examined. Let us say we are studying what kinds of intelligence are associated with scores on the Graduate Record Examination – Psychology Subject Test. Several hundred participants have been given an analytic intelligence test, a practical intelligence test, and an emotional intelligence test. We know that there is likely to be some overlap among the scores on these intelligence tests, and so we regress the participants' GRE–Psychology scores on to the three intelligence test scores and discover that the best "predictor" of GRE–Psychology scores is analytic intelligence. Now it is entirely possible that the correlations among the three intelligence tests are quite high, so that entering one of them in a regression model suppresses the influence of the other two. But if the zero-order correlations among the four constructs measured in this study are not presented prior to the multiple regression model, we cannot evaluate this alternative interpretation of the findings. So, as a general rule, a table of correlations should precede the reporting of regression analyses involving the same variables. Similarly, it is good form to report the internal consistency and/or the reliability of these kinds of measures before reporting the regression. A variable may look like an especially good "predictor" simply because it is the most reliably measured variable in the regression model. Remember the rule you learned in your statistics course: reliability limits validity.

A second example concerns the reporting of some measure of dispersion, usually standard deviation, before describing analyses, such as ANOVA, that are sensitive to the variance among measures. Generally, the table in which cell means are listed should also include standard deviations, so that the reader can eyeball the table and come up with pretty good effect size estimates before even looking to see if the ANOVA produced statistically significant results. The reader might also be interested in whether there is homogeneity of variance across measures and/or whether distributions of scores are more or less normal, all assumptions of general linear models that are often honored in the breach. Even if cell means are diagrammed in figures rather than reported in tables, it is generally considered good form to provide a sense of the distribution around these means using error bars based on standard errors or standard deviations.

A FEW OTHER ODDS AND ENDS

Finally, I will mention a few other rules of thumb for writing good Results sections. These are not hard-and-fast rules, but they will improve the clarity and impact of any article. Following them may also convey a sophistication about what you are doing with your data. The first set of tips concerns strategies for structuring the manuscript as a whole; the second set is focused more on the reporting of specific statistics.

Here are some tips concerning the organization of the manuscript:

1. In order to get to your main findings as quickly as possible, consider placing as many of the preliminaries in the Method section, such as the demographic breakdown of the sample, evidence that the participants were randomized to experimental conditions properly, and a sense that the cover story was believable and the measures reliable.

2. Put as much in tables and figures as possible. Although some editors may later force you to move material in tables and fig-

ures back to the text in order to save space in the printed journal, Results sections are usually more readable to the extent
that numbers are removed from the text itself. Always refer
explicitly to these tables and figures. It is not sufficient to note,
parenthetically at the end of a sentence, "(see Table 1)." Rather,
tell your readers what it is they can find in Table 1. For example:
"Table 1 lists the means and standard deviations for all of the
memory measures administered in this experiment. Comparing
the first and second columns of Table 1 reveals that for four of
the five variables, the quality and quantity of childhood memories differed for happy as compared to sad individuals."

3. Do not confuse redundancy with clarity. If means can be found
in a table, do not repeat them in the text itself or vice versa. You
don't need both a figure and a table illustrating the same finding.

4. Finally, consider a combined Results and Discussion section if
your manuscript is relatively short or if the Results are suffi-
ciently complex that detailed explanations along the way would
render them more intelligible.

Here are some tips about the reporting of actual statistics:

1. When reporting inferential statistics, provide complete information: the name of the test, the degrees of freedom or sample
size, the value of the test statistic, and whether it met the criterion you have set for statistical significance (Sternberg, 1988).

2. Don't make a fetish out of p-values. Generally, set an alpha level
or two in advance, such as $p < .05$ and $p < .01$, and report
whether a finding meets that criterion. It usually is not necessary to report exact levels of p. Moreover, reporting exact p-val-
ues conveys the impression that you think lower numbers mean
larger effect sizes, when this may not be the case (e.g., if the
sample sizes included in the test vary).

3. Don't feel obligated to report in detail every statistical approach
that you tried. For example, if you analyzed the data using several different transformations (e.g., log, reciprocal, square-root)
and the analyses always produced essentially the same findings,
feel free to tell the reader in a sentence or two (or even in a footnote) rather than present the same findings in different form

over and over again. The same rule holds when you try different factor extraction methods and rotations in a factor analysis, or different hierarchical approaches in a regression model.

4. Always try to describe your findings in the units actually measured, no matter how the data were analyzed. "Participants who first read positive words were 230 msec faster in responding to the target photograph than participants who first read negative words" is better than "Participants who first read positive words had faster reaction times (mean log RT = 2.27) to the photograph than participants who first read negative words (mean log RT = 3.89), $F(1, 38) = 6.21, p < .05$."

5. When statistical tests produce results that are not quite statistically significant, it is not necessary to qualify these findings with great barrages of defensive rhetoric, such as the results were "marginally significant," "did not reach conventional levels of significance," "just missed significance," "trended in the right direction," and so on. Rather, just state the claim, statistic, and p-value straightforwardly: "men smiled less often than women, $F(1, 203) = 3.70, p < .06$." The readers of your journal article can see that you "just missed" and can decide for themselves whether this shakes their confidence in your conclusions. At the same time, one should be especially careful to avoid overstatement in these situations (cf. Abelson, 1995, especially Chapter 4). Of course, some journal editors and reviewers feel that you are trying to slip something past them if you don't qualify a "nonsignificant" finding with some kind of adjective. If you believe this to be the case, then do it succinctly, such as by adding the word "somewhat" after "men smiled" in the example above, and move on without a lot of hemming and hawing.

THE BOTTOM LINE

I hope that I have persuaded you that the best Results section is written as a story. And like any good story, the author needs to establish a cast of characters and a setting, justify these selections, and then take the reader through the drama of steadily rising action, climax, and denouement. A good story is rarely a chronological rendition of every idea that occurred to the investigator as he or she stared at the data. In fact, the writing of the Results section (indeed, the article as a whole) may deviate sharply from the story that the investigator may have planned prior to actually conducting the study. As Bem (1987) so nicely puts it, "Scientific integrity does not require you to lead your readers through all your wrongheaded hunches only to show – *voila!* – they were wrongheaded. A journal article should not be a personal history of your stillborn thoughts" (p. 173) or, for that matter, a log of every statistical technique with which you whipped your data. Tell a good story, and let the drama of that story reveal itself through your results. "Think of your data as a jewel," Bem urges us. "Your task is to cut and polish it, to select the facets to highlight, and to craft the best setting for it" (p. 173).

REFERENCES

Abelson, R. P. (1995). *Statistics as principled argument.* Hillsdale, NJ: Erlbaum.
American Psychological Association. (1994). *Publication manual of the American Psychological Association.* Washington, DC: Author.
Bem, D. J. (1987). Writing the empirical journal article. In M. P. Zanna & J. M. Darley (Eds.), *The compleat academic* (pp. 171–201). New York: Random House.
Detweiler, J. B., Bedell, B. T., Salovey, P., Pronin, E., & Rothman, A. J. (1999). Message framing and sunscreen use: Gain-framed messages motivate beach-goers. *Health Psychology, 18,* 189–196.
Rothman, A. J., & Salovey, P. (1997). Shaping perceptions to motivate healthy behavior: The role of message framing. *Psychological Bulletin, 121,* 3–19.
Schank, R. C. (1990). *Tell me a story: A new look at real and artificial memory.* New York: Charles Scribner and Sons.
Singer, J. A., & Salovey, P. (1993). *The remembered self: Emotion and memory in personality.* New York: Free Press.
Sternberg, R. J. (1988). *The psychologist's companion.* Cambridge, England: Cambridge University Press.
Sternberg, R. J. (1998). *Love is a story.* New York: Oxford University Press.

Chapter 9

What Does It All Mean

The Discussion

ROBERT CALFEE

What can you say after you've said everything that you've already said? The *Publication Manual of the American Psychological Association* (APA, 1994) covers Discussion in a little over a page. The advice is to "evaluate and interpret . . . , examine and qualify . . . , and draw inferences from [the Results] . . . Emphasize any theoretical consequences . . . [and defend] the validity of your conclusions" (p. 18). You encounter three guiding questions:

- What have I contributed here?
- How has my study helped to resolve the original problem?
- What conclusions and theoretical implications can I draw from my study? (p. 19).

The *Publication Manual* offers a few thoughts about organizing the section; (a) open with a "clear statement of support or nonsupport for the original hypothesis," (b) link your findings with other work, (c) mention shortcomings (but don't flagellate yourself), and (d) speculate some but not too much. Finally, avoid repetitiveness, polemics, and triviality.

Relatively lean counsel. Surprisingly, most textbooks on research methods also say little or nothing about "Discussion." This chapter will attempt to fill this gap. Besides the *Publication Manual*, it draws on a variety of resources; a quick Internet check revealed more than a thousand entries on "Writing the research report," and that only scratched the surface. The Appendix annotates a few reference sources from my bookshelf. About my audience, I assume that you have recently completed a dissertation (not necessarily the best model for journal writing), and that you have a few things to say but are relatively new to the publishing game.

What does a Discussion look like? This question posed a challenge in designing this chapter. Reproducing entire segments was impossible, because Discussions are long. Presenting extracts would miss the point because the structure is what matters most.

A key word running throughout this chapter is *argument*. The next section examines the meaning of this concept. Next comes a section on substance and structure that describes how to *build* a case. The final section covers *style,* the devil in the details.

RESEARCH AS ARGUMENTATION

The essential starting points for composing a Discussion section are *purpose* and *audience*. Imagine that you are acting as a lawyer before an enormous panel of judges: other researchers, journal editors and reviewers, critics present and future. Earlier in your case you have set the stage and mustered evidence. Your concluding statement must now pull the pieces together, connect your claims with the data, defend against counterarguments and alternative interpretations, and convince the audience of the validity and value of your case.

Adopting an argumentative frame of mind takes some doing. From the elementary grades on you learned about "research" as routine detective work; a case is assigned, your job is to dig up the evidence and pass it on to the prosecutor. The aim is to report the right answer. Your doctoral experiences should have disavowed you of this view, but it still takes time to think like an authentic researcher. The Discussion quickly reveals an author's mindset. All too often a manuscript concludes "I found a problem, formed a hypothesis, collected data, did a statistical test, Q.E.D.!" Sorry, but it doesn't work that way. Science is not about finding right answers, but about questioning answers, no matter how well supported and commonsensical. That is why the doctoral candidate is required to *defend* the dissertation. This proceeding is not a final exam, but the beginning of a research career.

Formal arguments or debates follow principles. The first centers around the *building* of an argument. Toulmin (1958) laid out three foundation stones: *Claim* (or thesis), *Evidence* (or data), and *Warrant* (the connective tissue). You are familiar with the first two entries as the "beef" for the first sections of a research paper. Warrants, less familiar because schools seldom teach debating nowadays, aim to convince readers that the evidence supports the claim, and that no other interpretation is plausible. Recall the advice from the *Publication Manual* to "evaluate and interpret . . . , examine and qualify . . . , draw inferences;" this is what warrants are all about. To construct a warrant, you must move from your convictions (personal or otherwise) to the role of opposing counsel and attack your cherished conclusions. If the claim is fuzzy and the data weak or inconsistent, you clearly have a big job on your hands. But even when the evidence is clear and compelling (to you), critics will search for (and usually find) flaws in the methodology and alternative interpretations of the findings. So you must foresee assaults on your argument and be prepared to respond, even if it means changing your mind on occasion.

Validity offers a different way to think about argumentation. The distinction between internal and external validity should guide your thinking (Krathwohl, 1998, Section 3), although you may not use these labels. *Internal validity* refers to the coherence and consistency of your study. If you have not taken steps in designing the research to guard against confounded variables, poorly developed measures, and weak control over extraneous variability, then any interpretation of the results is undercut; the study lacks internal validity.

Value must also be weighed. Any single study, no matter how large and significant, is of value only as it generalizes to a broader range of situations; here is where *external validity* enters the picture. The Discussion is where writers most often argue for generalizability, sometimes accentuated and sometimes slipped in along the way. The attempt to generalize is often a minefield, especially when you have not thought the matter through. Large surveys may seem secure, but critics will ask for assurances of random and representative selection of the sample. More modest studies, especially those conducted with college sophomores in laboratory settings, present problems so widely recognized that they may appear to require no defense; readers automatically say to themselves, "Remember, this study may not apply to the real world." But most psychologists today take seriously terms such as *situated* and *contextualized* (Berliner & Calfee, 1996), and give greater credence to investigations grounded in authentic settings. Psychological research is more likely today to incorporate qualitative traditions and techniques (e.g., case studies and ethnographies), and researchers may explicitly disavow any intention to generalize the findings. But authors frequently stray from this commitment in the Discussion, where they implicitly or explicitly explore broader implications of the data. It is the natural thing to do! Psychological research, no matter the flavor, aims to generalize. The value of a study depends in part on how it informs other situations and settings. That is part of the argument.

A reminder: Keep the audience in mind. Think of the Discussion as a defense of the investigation. What message do you want to leave with the readers? You have spent months on the study; what are the two to four most significant points about the project? Lead with these in the Abstract, highlight them in the Results, punch them home at the beginning of the Discussion, develop them more fully in the body of the Discussion, and reiterate them in your concluding paragraphs. And you must do all of this without becoming repetitive. Think like a lawyer.

CONSTRUCTING A DISCUSSION

So much for mindset – now to the pragmatics. First you must get organized. Here is a sketch of a frequently used structure:

The Discussion section begins with an overview of the high priority findings, in reasonably plain English, and situated in the context of the original problem statement and the expected findings. Next work on the finer points: puzzling features in the data, inconsistent or unexpected findings, and mullings about what might have happened if you had changed the study ever so slightly. The Discussion links the findings to other literature and sketches the broader theoretical and practical implications. (after Calfee & Valencia, 1991, p. 12)

You may order the basic elements somewhat differently, but the recipe includes the main ingredients. The author presents research questions and hypotheses about the expected findings (the claim), and then moves through supporting evidence. The length and structure of the introduction of the Discussion depends on the complexity of the claim in relation to the findings. Readers may appreciate an overview paragraph: "The purpose of this study was to explore the hypothesis that____. I expected that____. The three most significant findings were____." Don't follow any formula in lockstep fashion; readers will be bored silly. But neither do you want to leave them guessing about the message; researchers encounter reams of reading, and do not have the luxury of dissecting creative expositions.

Focus the reader on the most significant and trustworthy outcomes. The reader has trudged through the Results section, often driven by methodology and containing substantial detail. In the Discussion you can (and should) step back from the trees and review the forest. Here is the place to present the high priority outcomes, to link these with the research problem and your hypotheses.

Following the overview, you should allocate one or more paragraphs to explore each point. The detailed structure of individual paragraphs will depend on the nature of the claim. If your findings confirm a well-established point in a different setting, you have one job to do; if the findings contradict previous research, that's another matter. You should have already built the case from previous literature, and you should reiterate only the most relevant works. Your task is to argue a series of mini-cases, during which your main job is to develop warrants.

The following frame provides one starting point:

Several findings support the conclusion that__ _BECAUSE____[the tough part, the warrant]. To be sure, the finding that_ __may seem inconsistent with the conclusion, BUT____[another part of the warrant]. And SoAndSo (19XX) has argued that____, BUT [yet another part of the warrant, and an example of a situation where you can legitimately return to the literature]."

Again, please don't copy this formula, but think of it as a first step toward laying out your argument. The Discussion is a time for honesty; "I expected X, but the most important finding turned out to be Y!" "When I began the study, I was convinced that finding A would support conclusion B, but on further reasoning I think that conclusions B or C are equally plausible."

One challenge is how to connect Results and Discussion. You need to prepare the reader for your conclusions but avoid over-interpretation in the Results. In the Discussion you shouldn't simply repeat the findings, but you need to summarize them in some fashion. Sternberg (1993) addresses this matter, noting that "a *Results* section standing by itself is difficult to follow and makes for dry reading . . . " (p. 53). But authors (guided by reviewers and editors, who are also part of the game) call for separation, fearing that data and interpretation may be muddled. Sternberg recommends "thematic links" between Results and Discussion, which makes sense. The aim is to give readers a "heads up" early on (preferably in the Introduction) about significant themes, and then to return to these themes along the way in Methods, Results, and finally Discussion.

The recommendation is that (a) results for multiple findings/studies include "links" to interpretative themes, (b) but that you clearly distinguish data from interpretation in the Results section (the focus here is evidence, not summation), and (c) that you cluster the Discussion around themes.

The *Publication Manual* suggests that you "emphasize theoretical consequences." Psychological theories still fall short of the grand themes found in the natural sciences, and a good deal of research aims toward practical outcomes. Does Program X lead to more valued outcomes than a control group?; What personological factors predict performance on a given task?; What is the correlation between measure A and measure B? And what about the empirical interactions among all of the above? Theory enters the picture when the researcher attempts to explain a collection of findings by a unified idea, a "grand claim." Tough and risky business. You must not only defend each particular point, but show how they support the larger conceptualization. Harp and Mayer (1998) refer to a "theory of cognitive interest," but they do not develop it at the outset, and give it only passing mention at the end of the Discussion.

Empirical studies sometimes solve practical problems, but time keeps changing the problems that are practical. Grounding a single investigation within a theoretical framework, more or less grand, is a difficult task. The most successful manuscripts that I have read occupy a middle ground. The researcher begins with a problem, connects it with one or more theoretical perspectives, explores the consequences of each, and then builds an "island," a small and delimited territory within which the theories can be put to a modest test. This strategy moves a study beyond strictly happenstance puzzlements ("I wonder what would happen if?") to a somewhat broader stage, but without attempting a Broadway opening.

One final remark about constructing a Discussion: Don't tell the story of how you conducted the research, unless it is absolutely vital to the argument. Young researchers sometimes express the sentiment that it is not "honest" to describe a study as though they knew at the outset what was going to happen. And they have a point. The manuscript, in both the Introduction and Discussion, should lay out your thinking as it occurred, even if this means admitting that things didn't come out as you predicted. But you don't need to personalize the account. "Based on several lines of work, I predicted that the outcome of the study would be____. The findings showed that____. A sensible interpretation of the results, in light of previous work, is____. The reasoning behind this argument is____."

STYLE THAT SUPPORTS SUBSTANCE AND STRUCTURE

In the previous section, I suggested that you divide your argument into distinctive chunks, decide which of those are most important, and then bring to bear the artillery of claim, evidence, and warrant. Sounds rather neat. But I have wandered into a minefield of my own making. I promised at the outset to discuss three points: the concept of argumentation, substance and structure, and style. You have just read a paragraph that combines all these elements in my cautionary note about the hazards of relying on a story for your argument because the substance and structure may be inappropriate, and the suggestion that you remedy this tension by stylistic adjustments. But the original advice still merits attention. If your thinking is muddled from beginning to end, then your paper will probably be muddled. Even if your thinking is crystal clear, however, you will still encounter muddy stretches along the way, sometimes because of stylistic problems.

The *Publication Manual* lists five topics under Style: Orderly Presentation of Ideas, Smoothness of Expression, Economy of

Expression, Precision and Clarity, and Strategies to Improve Writing Style. What a collection! And I will add a couple of items to the list. None of the chapters in the present volume addresses this topic, because all of them must handle it. So here is my advice for the role of style in the Discussion section. The *Publication Manual* allocates only a page or so to each topic, and you will need to call on other resources. Style takes a lifetime or more to acquire.

Orderly Presentation of Ideas

This is exactly the right starting point, and the focus of the present chapter. Lay out the main elements of your Discussion on scratch paper (or a computer scratch pad) before you begin serious writing. Don't worry about "order" at the outset; think instead about importance and persuasiveness. Arguments are generally more "psychological" than logical, which doesn't mean that standard logic does not apply, only that it does not suffice.

Smoothness of Expression

The *Publication Manual* makes several points under this heading, but the main message is "Don't surprise or confuse the reader." My recommendation that you begin the Discussion with an overview meshes with this advice. So does the Toulminian trio of Claim–Evidence–Warrant. Once you mentally ingrain this framework, you can guide readers through a consistent line of argument: "I want to convince you that X is the case. Here is the supporting evidence. Here is my explanation. Here are alternative explanations, and my defense against each of them." A stultifying style? Only if you follow it formulaically. Remember, you are lawyer more than novelist. To be sure, researchers who rely on case studies and ethnographies collect narrative data to support their claims. But scientific arguments cannot rely solely on the narrative genre for building the argument. Researchers must adopt a skeptical stance.

Surprise can serve a purpose on occasion. I recently read a paper on the positive effects of feedback on learning effectiveness. Like most readers, I assumed that feedback was a sure thing. The researchers led me down a garden path before suddenly confronting me with a substantial array of contradictory evidence. But rely on this tactic only when you have a sound reason for doing so.

Economy of Expression

"Say only what needs to be said" (*Publication Manual*, p. 26). Reading through the collection of Discussion sections that I accumulated in preparation for this chapter, my editorial pen wore calluses on my fingers. Shorten and sharpen. The *Publication Manual* identifies several culprits: jargon, wordiness, redundancy, long and complex sentences and paragraphs. Charge yourself by the word. And double the charge for sentences longer than 20 words.

Precision and Clarity

This section of the *Publication Manual* is one of my favorites, not only because it improves technical writing, but because it enhances communication across the board. The longest of the sections, it describes many ways to refine language: care in word choice, avoidance of ambiguity (the *indefinite this,* for instance), and the *royal we.* A sentence like "We think this is important to make it better" needs translation: "I think that this advice is important for strengthening a Discussion."

Interest (and Seduction?)

Missing from Style is any consideration of interest. Perhaps the assumption is that those who read research journals will plow through material no matter. And perhaps they will. But you can engage your audience more fully by infusing material that captures attention without diverting the flow of the argument; seductive "inducers" might actually assist comprehension. One technique is the inclusion of qualitative excerpts that illuminate quantitative findings. The idea is not to prove a claim, but to illustrate the meaning of the numbers.

Length

This is not the same as "Economy," and not included under Style. How long should a Discussion be? Long enough to say what you need to say, and no longer. A sound organization can save words, because it reduces redundancy. Ignoring trivialities also reduces length. What are the limitations of a study; as infinite as the stars of the winter sky! Too few informants, too few situations, not enough time, not enough money, and so on. Instead, go for your jugular; pick those matters that, on reflection, you view as significant insights that you gained from the experience. Writers often have problems ending a Discussion, perhaps because they aren't entirely clear about their main messages. So you will frequently find Conclusions, Summary, Implications, Final Thoughts, and Some Other Things, as the author desperately seeks to pin down the point of the study. Decide what's important, let the readers know about this decision at the outset, and you will find it easier to conclude the piece.

Strategies

This segment of the *Publication Manual* offers important advice, but mostly about grammar. Let me offer a different definition: strategy as *process*. Start with organization and emphasis. Decide how you want to structure the argument, how to begin and end, where to make your pitch, what caveats to include. Then write. Establish headings as mileposts, assemble paragraphs, shape sentences, fill the syntactic slots with the best words that come to mind. You are creating the clay from which the Discussion will eventually take shape. Once you have drafted a few pages on your word processor, let the material rest for a day or two. Much as dough needs to rise, so must your ideas ferment. The material will look different when you return to it. I typically read through the draft from the beginning, fixing little things along the way, but mostly regenerating the argument in my mind's eye. Sometimes you will make an important discovery – now that you have a rough draft, you realize what you really want to say! You may decide to turn the entire argument upside down, with implications for the entire work. Thank goodness for computers – this job used to be unbelievably onerous! Now I command the material; I can knead, mold, reformulate, with instant access to a thesaurus – what a wonderful world!

Tactics

This is another topic not found under Style. There finally comes a moment when I decide that the draft needs to be polished, which means (for me) a totally different mindset (for me), during which I focus on the "little pictures": Does this paragraph make sense, can this sentence be refined, is this the right word, do I need a citation at this point? It is a routinized process, during which I focus on minute details, focusing on one screen at a time. When I was in college, I worked as a short-order cook in a drive-in restaurant. After filling each order, I erased it from memory and went on to the next slip, quite unlike Julia Child planning a grand party. As a writer, you need to move back and forth between these roles, sometimes framing the big picture, other times the artisan refining details. Some writers seem to "parallel process"; I cannot, nor can most novices. Be patient.

CONCLUSION

While preparing this chapter, I have reflected on the decision-making demands from various sections of a research paper. Your choices are limited in some sections. The reference section is pretty automatic, albeit a pain. The Abstract is difficult to construct, but tightly constrained. Parenthetically, APA policy calls for a "conclusions-oriented" abstract, which means that you must compress the substance of the Discussion into a couple of sentences. Methods and Results can vary widely, but you know what you have to do.

The Introduction and the Discussion – these bookends shape the research question and lay out the research "answer." Tough sections, in that they call for genuinely original thinking. I have attempted in this chapter to provide you with a theme (Discussion as argumentation), a few frameworks, a handful of examples, along with strategic and tactical approaches. But this is hard work; find a few good models and think about them. Also remember the *Publication Manual's* guiding questions presented at the beginning of the chapter: What have you contributed to understanding the original problem, conceptually and practically? Leave your audience with a clear image about your answer to this fundamental question.

APPENDIX: A SHORT LIST OF ANNOTATED SOURCES FOR COMPOSING AN ARGUMENT

You can find literally hundreds of books on research and report writing at any of the bookstores on the World Wide Web. Many of these aim at the undergraduate market, and you have hopefully moved beyond this level. A popular tactic is the "N-Step" approach; the number of steps ranges from 8 to more than 35! Other texts are more specialized (e.g., ethnographies and case studies).

Some textbooks on research methods offer advice on research writing (e.g., Krathwohl, 1998, includes an appendix on writing the research proposal), but not all (e.g., Gall, Borg, & Gall, 1996). So what can you call upon other than the *Publication Manual?* Here are four suggestions that I have chosen because (a) they are readable, (b) they help me *think* about how to write, and (c) they are reasonably recent. Three of the four books offer broad coverage; they speak as much to the historian as the social scientist.

Barzun, J., & Graff, H. F. (1992). *The modern researcher* (5th ed.). New York: Harcourt Brace. As described by the publisher, this updated classic is "three manuals in one": (a) advice on how to collect and assess information about a topic, (b) counsel about clear, well-organized, and jargon-free language, and (c) instructions for refining a paper for both publication and oral presentation.

Booth, W. C., Williams, J. M., & Colomb, G. G. (1995). *The craft of research.* Chicago, IL: University of Chicago Press. Another updated classic, which focuses on the process of constructing a research paper. It gives explicit attention to argumentation, and to the elements of claim, evidence, and warrant. An excellent reference source.

Sternberg, R. J. (1993). *The psychologist's companion* (ed. III). Cambridge, England: Cambridge University Press. A small and handy reference focused on psychology and social science. Well worth the investment for novice and experienced writer alike.

Zinsser, W. K. (1998). *On writing well: An informal guide to writing non-fiction.* New York: HarperCollins. My all-time favorite for readability; Zinsser's style is engaging but informative. He begins by connecting with the beginning writer, who has probably never composed for a "real" audience, and then coaxes you into the different styles of thinking required by various types of expository writing. The book begins with principles, which include such terms as *the transaction, simplicity, clutter, style, the audience,* which should resonate. He then turns to *forms and methods,* in which he tailors the principles to a range of writing tasks, from "The Travel Memoir" to "Sports," but including "Science and Technology" and "Business Writing." Highly recommended.

REFERENCES

American Psychological Association, (1994). *Publication manual of the American Psychological Association* (4th ed.). Washington, DC: Author.

Berliner, D. C. & Calfer, R. C. (Eds.) (1996) *Handbook of educational psychology.* New York: Macmillan.

Calfee, R. C. & Valencia, R. R. (1991). *APA Guide to preparing manuscripts for publication.* Washington, D. C.: American Psychological Association.

Gall, M. D., Borg, W. R., & Gall, J. P. (1996). *Educational research: An introduction* (6th ed.). White Plains, NY: Longman.

Harp, S. F., & Mayer, R. E. (1998). How seductive details do their damage: A theory of cognitive interest in science learning. *Journal of Educational Psychology, 90,* 414–434.

Krathwohl, D. R. (1998). *Methods of educational and social science research: An integrated approach* (2nd ed.). New York: Longman.

Sternberg, R. J. (1993). The psychologist's companion (Ed. III). Cambridge: Cambridge University Press.

Toulmin, S. E. (1958). *The uses of argument.* New York: Cambridge University Press.

Chapter 10

Documenting Your Scholarship

Citations and References

RANDOLPH A. SMITH

I would be surprised if this is the first chapter you examine in this book; in fact, I would be surprised if this chapter is in the first few you examine. Dealing with citations and references in a manuscript is not typically what one thinks of as a "glamorous" or exciting topic. It is, however, one of the most important topics regarding manuscript preparation because through citations and references you make or break your reputation as a careful and thorough scholar. Readers will evaluate how you used citations and references to provide background information for your topic, to develop a clear and convincing hypothesis, and to buttress your arguments. In addition, other readers will use your references to track down material they wish to explore. Thus, readers, including editors and reviewers, will use and evaluate your citations and references for a variety of purposes. For these reasons, careful scholarship is a must. Dunn (1999, p. 89) maintained that a reference section is as important in scholarly communication as is the remainder of one's paper. According to Sternberg (1988, p. 56), "Incorrect citations are a disservice to readers and show sloppy scholarship." Finally, Bruner (1942, p. 68) noted

a sin one more degree heinous than an incomplete reference is an inaccurate reference; the former will be caught by the editor or printer, whereas the latter will stand in print as an annoyance to future investigators and a monument to the writer's carelessness.

146

This point is important enough that the *Publication Manual of the American Psychological Association* (APA, 1994, p. 175) includes a portion of this quote. It is clear, then, that you should take great care with your text citations and your reference list in any manuscript you compose.

As a journal editor *(Teaching of Psychology)*, I process a large number of manuscripts and have noted recurrent problems with citations and references. Many of the problems are mechanical errors in making citations and listing references. I have encountered virtually no mechanical problems that authors could not solve by referring to the relevant pages in the *Publication Manual*. The major problem appears to be that authors simply do not consult the *Publication Manual*. My primary advice: When you have a question concerning a citation or reference, *consult the Publication Manual!* You will be dealing with a rare situation indeed if you cannot find an answer therein. Of course, the goal for this book is to go beyond the rules and regulations of the *Publication Manual* and to provide helpful advice for writers. Let me give you some pointers I have gleaned from my work as a journal editor. My comments fall into four categories: major offenses, minor errors, plagiarism, and future issues.

MAJOR OFFENSES

My experiences and practices as an editor may not exactly match those of any other editor. From talking to other editors, however, I believe that there are some situations that plague us regardless of the journal (or other publication outlet) involved. The problems I classify here as major offenses are citation and reference problems so severe that I may reject a manuscript solely on their basis.

The Necessity of References

Few research studies, ideas, or opinions are so original that they require no background references (and the accompanying citations). I believe this statement to be true even in publication outlets that allow for opinion pieces and the like. If authors submit a manuscript with no references, most editors and reviewers may react as they do to some student papers that they categorize as "shooting from the hip." Is it truly the case that papers with no references are a common problem? Probably not. But it is an extreme example of a somewhat common problem – the error of skimpy referencing.

Often, writers submit manuscripts in which it appears they have presented the smallest amount of background literature possible. Faced with such a situation, an editor (or reviewer) is uncertain whether the writer was merely being economical, was unfamiliar with the literature, or might even be guilty of plagiarism. I routinely read multiple-sentence passages and paragraphs without citations. Thus, it is common for me to ask authors for additional citations and references. Rarely must I ask them to cull citations and references.

I believe that the problem of skimpy referencing is often due to the confusion that authors have in knowing whether to provide a citation. Unfortunately, there is no hard-and-fast rule about when to cite a source and when not. The *Publication Manual* is vague on this issue, saying only "document your study throughout the text by citing by author and date the works you researched" (p. 168). The *Publication Manual* also tells you to assume that your readers have some background knowledge (p. 11). Smyth (1996, p. 46) advised using the following rule: "If you make a statement that you could reasonably expect an intelligent reader to believe, there is no need to provide supporting evidence." Although Smyth's guideline is more specific than APA's, it raises the difficulty of discerning who constitutes an "intelligent reader." With the increasing specialization of many journals, the pool of intelligent readers may be getting smaller and smaller. Often, readers without the background in a specific research area will not be totally familiar with the extant literature. Dunn (1999) provided a list of four questions to ask yourself (see Table 1). If the answer to any of the questions is yes, Dunn suggested citing the source. In my attempt to derive a guiding principle about whether to include a citation, I agree with the advice of Jolley, Murray, and Keller (1984) to err on the side of caution and provide citations if you have any question about whether the reader would believe your statement without evidence. Part of your job as a scholar is to document the evidence, so providing citations and references is a desirable behavior.

Table 1. Questions to Determine Whether to Include a Citation

Was any scientific fact, hypothesis, or definition from the reference used?
Were any ideas from the reference used to shape your thinking about the theory used in your project?
Did you borrow or adapt any methodology from a reference for your project?
Did you use the same statistical tests or other analytic procedures discussed in the reference?

From *The practical researcher: A student guide to conducting psychological research*, by D. Dunn, 1999, Boston: McGraw-Hill, p. 89.

Having just encouraged you to cite references freely, I now make a disclaimer. It is not your task in writing a manuscript to cite every relevant published reference. Some discretion is necessary on this count. The *Publication Manual* (p. 11) specifically notes that the literature review is not meant to be "exhaustive." Thus, the writer must walk a narrow path – being sure to cite important and relevant information, but being careful not to cite too much. As you read other writers' introductions, pay attention to their citation/reference strategy and learn from them. My experience suggests many more writers undercite than overcite.

The Necessity of Current References

Now that you are prepared to provide relevant references to serve as background information, you should address the recency of those references. Part of the responsibility of being a scholar is staying current in the field. I am surprised at the frequency with which I receive manuscripts that have no references published within the last few years. Does this lack of current references mean that the author is pursuing a "dead" line of research or that the writer is simply not up-to-date on the recent literature? Neither conclusion is a good one to reach.

Today, there is little excuse for being behind the times on the research literature in a given area. With increasing access to computerized databases for searching and obtaining articles, e-mail access to most researchers around the world, on-line journals, World Wide Web searches, and research-oriented home pages, it is difficult to use one's limited library holdings or isolated geographic location as excuses for using outdated research literature. Indeed, the complaint of today may well be that one has access to too much information rather than too little.

I do not mean for my emphasis on current references to imply that older references are not important. Often, older references at the beginning of an introduction serve to provide a historical context for your writing. Typically, however, your citations will be to newer and newer articles as you get closer to the description of your work. If your particular work is based on old information, you may have missed some important milestones. In such a case, the citations and references in your manuscript will be a clear indicator of whether you are submitting work that is current or already dated.

The Necessity of Relevant References

After reading this section heading, you may have thought that the necessity of providing relevant references is an obvious point. You are correct – to some extent. Surely it is unlikely that anyone would provide references to work on neurophysiology in a manuscript dealing with Freud's id, ego, and superego. Although an example such as this one may be relatively obvious, I have three examples of other types of relevance that are less obvious.

Impartial Relevance. Researchers have an ethical obligation to be fair with the evidence. This type of fairness means that you should not cite information that supports only your position and ignore other information. It is important to give both (or all) sides of the story in order to remain fair and impartial. Authors, of course, do have biases and theoretical leanings. Still, it is your responsibility to strive for impartiality in your written presentations. Editors may wonder about the impartiality of authors who cite only their own publications as supporting evidence.

Evidential Relevance. Lalumière (1993) maintained that different types of citations perform different functions. He was primarily concerned with citations used to support a position or statement rather than simply providing sources for information. Lalumière said that supportive citations could fall into four categories: (a) opinion, (b) literature review, (c) results from an empirical study, and (d) meta-analyses. He argued that only the latter two were truly empirical and that authors should be careful to cite empirical work if at all possible. Thus, Lalumière argued that authors should use only results from empirical studies or meta-analyses as true supportive evidence. He noted, however, that authors often use nonempirical citations to support ideas that actually need empirical support.

Of course, it is sometimes the case that writers must use nonempirical information because there is simply no empirical support available. In such cases, I would point out that authors should be aware of the limitations of their supporting information. Do not make claims that outstrip the strength of your evidence to support those claims. Also, in such cases, the *Publication Manual* (p. 20) instructs authors to make it clear that they are citing nonempirical work.

Journal Relevance. When you submit a manuscript to a journal, there is an implicit presumption that you have evaluated that manuscript and the type of material published in the journal and that you see the two as compatible. If the manuscript and journal are compatible, it stands to reason that past issues of the journal would contain articles relevant to your manuscript. I continue to be surprised at the number of manuscripts I receive that deal with teaching of psychology in some way but that do not contain any references from *Teaching of Psychology*. From the responses of many of the reviewers for the journal, they apparently also find that absence surprising. If your work does not contain any references from the journal to which you submitted, the editor and reviewers may again wonder if you have "done your homework." I would not argue that every published article should have a reference to another article in the same journal, but I would hazard a guess that the vast majority do. If you are unable to find any relevant information in a particular journal, then it may be that that journal is not one you should consider for the manuscript you are preparing.

MINOR ERRORS

I realize that there is a risk in labeling a problem of any sort as a "minor error." In using this label, I do not mean that these errors are inconsequential or that authors should ignore these problems. In my editorial work, this label simply means that I would not reject a manuscript solely on the basis of problems such as these. I would, however, view them as problems that need attention. My hunch is that editors who see errors such as these would make attributions about the writer such as "sloppy attention to detail."

Citations and References Should Match

Although there are numerous books to assist faculty and students in writing APA-style papers, few of them include much information about citations and references. There is, however, one notable exception. Without fail, such books stress that the citations in text and the reference list should match (e.g., Jolley et al., 1984; Rosnow & Rosnow, 1998; Smyth, 1996; Sternberg, 1988). Simply put, this admonishment means that you should provide references for *all* citations and cite *all* references in the body of the paper. I encounter many manuscripts with a text citation for which there is no reference, a reference for which there is no text citation, and text citations and references for which the dates or spellings of authors' names do not match. Checking for agreement of citations and references is a simple matter, but one that many authors neglect.

A related point to this section is the rule that, in APA style, authors compile a reference list, not a bibliography. Unlike some styles that English teachers use, psychologists do not list all works consulted in the reference list. Only if you cite a source in the text do you list it as a reference.

Citations and References Should Be Accurate

When I check a reference list for a submitted manuscript, I check as many references as possible against the original sources. I find enough errors that I have a standard line in my letters to authors that asks them to recheck their references. Apparently no references are immune from error; I have seen numerous writers make errors in referencing articles they authored. Here's a simple rule: Do not trust your memory! No matter how many times you have previously typed a reference, look up the *original* source when you type it in your reference list.

Avoid Secondary Citations

I suspect that many errors in referencing (see previous section) come about because of relying on secondary citations. It is tempting to read about Author B's work in Author A's article and to simply copy A's reference to B's work. The problem that occurs when authors adopt this strategy is that they must rely on Author A's accuracy in referencing Author B. I imagine that most people reading this chapter have had several experiences of going to the library to look up a reference you found in some source, only to find that the reference was incorrect and you could not locate the article you wanted. Thus, there is ample evidence that errors in referencing exist in the published literature. Why trust a secondary source to get a reference correct for your published work? If there is an error in that reference, the negative reflection will be on you and your work, not on the long-forgotten author from whom you got the incorrect reference.

Prytula, Oster, and Davis (1977) demonstrated the effects of using secondary sources when they surveyed several introductory psychology and learning textbooks' coverage of Watson and Rayner's work with Little Albert. They found that the texts had many details of Watson and Rayner's work wrong. For example, although Watson and Rayner used a live white rat for Albert's initial conditioning, the texts referred to a toy white rat, a toy or pet animal, or a rabbit. Also, many of the sources reported that Watson and Rayner extinguished Little Albert's fear, which actually did not occur. Goodwin (1991) also showed the problems of secondary citations when he found that the typical picture in introductory psychology texts allegedly portraying Pavlov's apparatus for classically conditioning dogs was much more sophisticated than Pavlov's. Rather, the illustration was more like equipment that Nicolai used.

It is important that you are honest if you *do* use secondary citations. Rather than making an apparent claim that you read an article, cite the primary source you read that included the secondary source (APA, 1994, pp. 200–201). Thus, if there is an error of interpretation, it will rest on your primary source rather than appearing to be your error. Similarly, if you read only the abstract of a published study (whether from an original or secondary source), you should include that information in your reference (APA, 1994, pp. 198–199).

PLAGIARISM

The *Publication Manual* (pp. 292–294) mentions the issue of plagiarism briefly under the heading "Ethics of Scientific Publication." That coverage derives from the APA's *Ethical Principles* (1992), which covered plagiarism thusly: "Psychologists do not present substantial portions or elements of another's work or data as their own, even if the other work or data source is cited occasionally" (Standard 6.22, p. 1609). Thus, an ethical writer does not quote from another with making proper attribution. As Dunn (1999) noted (see Table 1), ethical writers should give credit as well for ideas that come from other authors.

Perhaps the most difficult concept involving plagiarism is that of paraphrasing. According to the *Publication Manual*, "each time a source is paraphrased, a credit for the source needs to be included in the text" (pp. 292, 294). This standard changes the ethicality of a practice many writers have used since childhood – changing a word or a few words to avoid quoting a source. According to the *Publication Manual* and many authors' interpretations (e.g., Allen, 1995; Dunn, 1999; Slade, 1997; Smith, 1995; Smyth, 1996), that writing style is considered plagiarism, even if you provide a citation. Changing only a word here and there still means that you have stolen that author's thoughts. To help emphasize this point to writers, Slade (1997, pp. 55–58) differentiated between "direct quotation" and "indirect quotation." She used the term indirect quotation to refer to passages that authors restate in their own words. If writers remember the concept of indirect quotations, it should help them avoid plagiarism that they might otherwise commit inadvertently.

FUTURE ISSUES

It is usually risky to write about the future because your words have a way of coming back to haunt you. Nonetheless, I will cover two topics that may well impact the future of citations and references in writing.

World Wide Web References

There is little doubt that authors will use growing numbers of citations and references from the World Wide Web (Web) in coming years. The growth of the Web in the past few years has been phenomenal. Just a few years ago, few people could have predicted how wide-spread the availability of information on the Web would be. Unfortunately, the newest revision of the *Publication Manual* came out just as the Web was gaining in popularity. In fact, there is an admission in the *Publication Manual* (p. 218) that a standard reference format for Web information had not yet evolved. Although the *Publication Manual* provided a template for such references, I find that this format is not adequate.

Instead, I urge authors to use an updated reference format from APA's home page (APA, 1999). This newer reference format (e.g., see my references to APA, 1999, and Smith, 1995) provides the basic information just as you would for printed sources. Of course, the reference also provides the Web address where you accessed the document. In addition, this format includes a second date: the date that you actually accessed the document. Readers have simple indicators to alert them to revised printed material through notice of new editions. On the Web, however, edition numbers are not used. Thus, a Web site could be edited dramatically (or cease to exist) from the time you accessed it, leaving a reader frustrated in trying to find the material you cited. Because you provide your access date in your reference, this information can help the reader realize that the site's content may have changed since you accessed it. One additional caution is in order. I urge you to check this site on APA's Web page on a periodic basis for updates. As I was writing this chapter, I found a slight change in the recommended format.

Bibliographic Software

In recent years, software manufacturers have developed software that could make using citations and references a simpler process. Older versions of such programs were not much more than bibliography holding programs – you could use them to create lists of references, something you could do as easily with a word-processing program. Newer versions of bibliographic software, however, seem to have the potential for assisting authors in making the citation and reference process simpler. I recently received ad copy concerning a particular bibliographic program. According to the advertising, this program goes far beyond a simple cataloging process. For example, it allows you to search databases on the Web and transfer the results of those searches to your computer in the bibliographic program. After you insert relevant citations in your document, the program will create your reference list for you. As you can imagine, having a tool such as this could make the citation/reference process easier and more accurate.

A FINAL WORD

As I mentioned in my introductory paragraphs, I have resisted the temptation to quote chapter and verse from the *Publication Manual*. Instead, I have tackled what I see as the larger issues concerning citations and references and have left it for you to read carefully the *Publication Manual* for the nuts and bolts information you need. Let me pass along one last word of advice: If you have any obsessive-compulsive tendencies at all, let them take over – they will serve you well as you deal with citations and references. Remember that readers will view your citations and references as an important element of your scholarship.

ACKNOWLEDGMENT

I appreciate the help of Stephen Davis, Jane Halonen, David Johnson, and Randall Wight, who read an early draft of this chapter and offered suggestions.

REFERENCES

Allen, M. J. (1995). *Introduction to psychological research.* Itasca, IL: Peacock.
American Psychological Association. (1992). Ethical principles of psychologists and code of conduct. *American Psychologist, 47,* 1597–1611.
American Psychological Association. (1994). *Publication manual of the American Psychological Association* (4th ed.). Washington, DC: Author.
American Psychological Association. (1999). *Electronic reference formats recommended by the American Psychological Association* [Announcement]. Washington, DC: Author. Retrieved December 31, 1999 from the World Wide Web: http://www.apa.org/journals/webref.html
Bruner, K. F. (1942). Of psychological writing: Being some valedictory remarks on style. *Journal of Abnormal and Social Psychology, 37,* 52–70.
Dunn, D. S. (1999). *The practical researcher: A student guide to conducting psychological research.* Boston: McGraw-Hill.

Goodwin, C. J. (1991). Misportraying Pavlov's apparatus. *American Journal of Psychology, 104*, 135–141.

Jolley, J. M., Murray, J. D., & Keller, P. A. (1984). *How to write psychology papers: A student's survival guide for psychology and related fields.* Sarasota, FL: Professional Resource Exchange.

Lalumière, M. L. (1993). Increasing the precision of citations in scientific writing. *American Psychologist, 48*, 913.

Prytula, R. E., Oster, G. D., & Davis, S. F. (1977). The "rat rabbit" problem: What did John B. Watson really do? *Teaching of Psychology, 4*, 44–46.

Rosnow, R. L., & Rosnow, M. (1998). *Writing papers in psychology: A student guide* (4th ed.). Pacific Grove, CA: Brooks/Cole.

Slade, C. (1997). *Form and style: Research papers, reports, theses* (10th ed.). Boston: Houghton Mifflin.

Smith, P. C. (1995). *Establishing authorship.* Retrieved October 18, 1998 from the World Wide Web: http://www.uwm.edu/people/pcsmith/author1.htm

Smyth, T. R. (1996). *Writing in psychology: A student guide* (2nd ed.). New York: Wiley.

Sternberg, R. J. (1988). *The psychologist's companion: A guide to scientific writing for students and researchers* (2nd ed.). Cambridge, England: Cambridge University Press.

PART THREE

DEALING WITH REFEREES

Chapter 11

Writing for Your Referees

ROBERT J. STERNBERG

The best psychological journals share relatively few attributes. Some contain only empirical articles; others contain no empirical articles. Some publish only short articles; others publish only long articles. Some encourage free submissions; others are by invitation only. One thing these journals have in common, however, is that the articles submitted to them are refereed: The articles go through a process of peer review before a decision is made as to their fate.

One way to improve your chances of getting your articles accepted is to *write with your future referees in mind*. In writing and then reading over your article, think the way your referees will think. Writing with referees in mind substantially, even drastically, improves chances of a favorable outcome for your article. So many of the rejections authors receive easily could have been averted had those authors written with their future referees in mind. This article contains a dozen tips on how to improve your chances of acceptance by writing with the referees in mind.

1. *Proofread.* The simplest thing you can do is to proofread your article before you submit it. Referees rarely reject articles solely because they are chock full of typographical, grammatical, or word-processing errors. But such errors severely irritate most referees and are likely to put them into a rejecting frame of mind. Thus, the referees are likely to magnify the importance of other flaws and then to recommend that your article get the axe. Probably they are hoping you get it too.

This punitive frame of mind is easily understandable. Referees are donating time as a professional service. Almost all of them would rather be doing something else. They donate the time because they want their articles refereed, and the only way the system will work is if they give in exchange for what they hope to get. But referees do not want to be proofreaders. If they did, they would have chosen proofreading as a career, or they would have become high school English teachers.

Their feeling in reading an article is likely to be that if the author did not want to bother to proofread his or her article, then they should not be obliged to review it. In my experience, lack of proofreading is the easiest thing to fix but one of the things that least often actually is fixed.

There are several reasons why many authors do not proofread their articles. None of the reasons is good.

First, authors may think their word processor did what they, the authors, should have done. The trouble is that the spell checker is of no help for spelling errors that constitute real words, as when *principal* is spelled as *principle,* or for when the word that is used is correctly spelled but simply inappropriate. Grammar checkers don not always function correctly either. For example, the previous sentence passed both my spell checker and my grammar checker with flying colors, despite its containing a blatant error.

Second, reading their own articles may make authors anxious. Sometimes they are appalled by what they read. But imagine how the referees must feel. They did not even write the thing, so it is worse for them.

Third, authors may think that they do not have the time to proofread. But is it fair to expect referees and editors to do what authors do not want to bother themselves to do? Of course not. So proofread your article before submitting it! Look for spelling errors, grammar and capitalization errors, errors in usage, and for missing or out-of-order pages or tables or figures. Also check that the references match the citations in the text of the article. Proofreading also gives you one more chance to check the facts and the accuracy of what you wrote.

2. *Ask one or more trusted colleagues to read the article the way a referee would.* Did you ever find an obvious typographical error in a published article and wonder how the author could have missed it?

The answer is that the author missed it the same way you would have. After reading the darn thing several times, the author kept seeing the error without encoding it as an error.

In general, we experience a certain habituation to our own work, the same way others do. It is much like a dirty or messy house. What looks dirty or messy to an outsider has come to look clean and neat to the person who lives in the dump. It often takes an outsider to spot things that will be obvious to everyone except the person who wrote the article.

3. *State clearly the problem you are addressing and then organize the article around the problem.* Sometimes it is hard to figure out exactly what problem the author of an article thought he or she was trying to solve. This phenomenon can occur because the author does not know what problem the article is supposed to solve, or because the nature of this problem was not clearly communicated. It is the author's responsibility to make clear early in the article what problem or problems the article tackles.

Once you have stated the problem, organize the article around it. Show why the problem is important — why it should matter to anyone beside you. If you do not know, why should a referee? In the literature review, use relevance to the problem tackled as the major basis for deciding what to cite. In the methods section, make clear how the methods address the problem. In the results section, tell the story of how the successive analyses help solve the problem that was originally posed. And then, in the discussion section, summarize what you did and discuss its implications.

A clearly focused, tightly organized article has a great advantage in the review process. You are helping the referee understand what your goals are and how you are trying to reach them. If you leave it to the referees to figure these things out, there is a good chance that the conclusions they come to will differ from your own.

4. *Cite likely referees (who conceivably merit citation).* Suppose I consider myself one of the world's greatest experts on the effects of high-fat, sugary foods on amorous behavior. I view myself as one of the few people who really knows what happens subsequently when romantically involved couples go out on a date and share a large piece of cheesecake. I get an article to review on the topic and look forward to reading it. First, of course, I check the references to see which of my superlative articles on this topic have been cited. I discover that none of them are cited. I cannot believe it. How could anyone write about this topic without citing my work? I now start reading the article, but I already know it is a pretty poor piece with awful scholarship. All I need to do is find some reason to reject it, and I most likely will.

It is impossible to anticipate everyone who might referee an article. Nor can one cite every potential reviewer. But it is important to cite likely referees who have made a serious contribution to work in the field that the article covers. And if the editor has sent the article to a particular reviewer, the editor, at least, considers the individual to be one of the more active contributors to the field the article covers. Thus, this suggestion is not a cynical one: The likely referees are the same people who are likely to be the major contributors to the field.

5. *Make clear up front what the new and valuable contribution of your article is, and make sure you are right.* My conversations with journal editors suggest that the #1 reason for rejection of journal articles is lack of substance – there just is not enough new in the article to justify its publication in their journal. Reviewers, too, are on the lookout for articles that have little or nothing new to say.

It therefore behooves you to ask yourself what the new and valuable contribution of your article is, and to make clear near the beginning of the article what it is. Do not expect reviewers to figure it out for themselves. If you cannot figure it out, you cannot expect them to. If you cannot find such a contribution, either do more research or do more thinking before you submit the article.

6. *Make clear how your work builds on that of others.* No one likes a credit hog – someone that makes a contribution and then acts as though no one else has ever had any idea of value in the area of work. Sharing credit goes beyond citing potential reviewers. It involves showing how your work builds on their work and the work of many others. Scholarship always requires drawing connections between what is new and what is old.

It also is important in citing references that you are up-to-date. Referees generally are not happy to see reference lists that would have been up-to-date a decade earlier. So check recent literature in the area in which you are working. In this way, you also are less likely to repeat what someone already has done.

Some authors may feel that, in setting out in a bold new direction, they really owe almost nothing to anybody else. But it is important to realize that, even when you oppose old ideas, you still are using those ideas as a base from which to map your campaign of opposition. And even when you move away from what others have done, had they not done what they had done, you would not have had their work to move away from. Thus it is important to show how you build on, not just how you go beyond, past work.

7. *Check your data analyses and interpretations.* If your article makes a substantial contribution, there is a good chance that someone will ask for your data, which you are obliged to provide to him or her. This "someone" may be a referee, or someone who later reads the article. One of the more embarrassing events in the life of an academic is to have one's data analyses demolished. It is therefore important to check that you have used the correct forms of analysis and to ensure that you have transcribed the statistics correctly.

Also make sure that your interpretations are correct. For example, more stringent levels of significance do not indicate stronger effects, but rather, lesser likelihoods that a given result would have been obtained under the null hypothesis.

8. *Make sure that your conclusions follow from your data.* High up on the list of annoyances to referees is the author whose claims go well beyond his or her data. Such authors are all too common. They may have a modest finding and then write about that finding as though they have changed the face of the earth. If your conclusions go beyond your data, chances are that referees will notice this fact and lash out at the conclusions and at you.

There is a place in most articles for speculation that goes beyond the boundaries of the data. This place is in the Discussion section of the article. But when you go beyond the boundaries of the data, make clear that you are speculating. Do not assume that referees or other readers will know that you know you are in a speculative state of mind.

9. *Explain things clearly and in sufficient but not excessive detail.* It is annoying to a referee to be unable to judge some aspect of the work because that aspect is not clearly explained. The referee should not have to spend a lot of time trying to figure out what you really wanted to say. Make sure you say it and say it clearly. When you describe past work, describe it in sufficient detail so that someone unfamiliar with this work can nevertheless get the idea without having to go back to that work. When you explain what you did, explain it in sufficient detail so that someone else could replicate what you did precisely.

Novice article-writers often fall into one of two traps. These traps are of too much and too little detail.

The dissertation trap is to go into such great detail that readers can barely stay awake trying to sort the wheat from the chaff. Keep the mind-numbing details to dissertations rather than articles for published journals. If you need to go into considerable detail, write hierarchically so that the main ideas shine through. Do not force referees or other readers to get hopelessly mired in a bog of turgid writing from which they cannot escape.

The other trap is to assume that every reader has the detailed knowledge of a specialized area that the writer of the article has. Relatively few people will have your knowledge about your own area of specialization. Moreover, most readers, when confused, will not try to puzzle out what you really meant to say. Why should they bother? Chances are good that they will give up on your article. Many referees will simply say that it is impossible adequately to judge the article. Even if they keep reading, they are likely to regard you as muddle-headed or as the poor writer you have shown yourself to be.

10. *Anticipate likely objections to your interpretations of the data.* Confirmation bias seems to be a matter of human nature. But just as you read your own data through your preferred lenses, so do your referees. And they may be wearing different lenses from yours. It is important to anticipate likely objections to your interpretations and to defuse these objections before your intellectual opponents ever set their eyes on your article.

Having an intellectual opponent read the article before you submit it is one way to anticipate objections. Another way is to put yourself in the place of the opposition, and ask yourself how your opponents might interpret the data in a way that would render the data most favorable to their own oppositional point of view. Then show, in your Discussion section, why their interpretation cannot be correct. Or if it can be correct, at least acknowledge this fact. If the data are inconclusive, however, your article may be rejected for this reason. Thus, if you realize that your data are inconclusive, you might wish to wait to submit the article until you have done further research.

Editors often deliberately send articles for review to referees who are likely to be predisposed not to accept the conclusions of the article. Good editors take into account not only what reviewers say, but also, who said it. But not all editors are good, and some treat the words of reviewers as divine revelations, no matter how idiotic what they say may be. Other bad editors seem never to read any of the articles submitted to them, so they have no choice but to accept what the reviewers say.

You have to hope that the editors with whom you deal do not simply take at face value everything the reviewers say. Fortunately, there are many competent editors. Unfortunately, the number of incompetent ones is not vanishingly small.

It occasionally happens that there is someone out there in the wilds who, you believe, has a personal animosity against you that goes beyond intellectual disagreement. When you submit an article, you can request that a particular individual not referee your article. If you do so, you should say why, and realize that it is up to the editor to decide whether he or she will honor your request. You also can suggest referees, although the editor is under no obligation whatsoever to accept any of your suggestions.

11. *Make clear what the limitations of your work are.* Any good Discussion section includes at least some frank acknowledgment of the limitations of the study. Did you use just a single methodology, or type of stimulus material? Did you use a restricted range of types of participants? Did you look at behavior only in one kind of situation, perhaps an artificially contrived one? Referees and all readers appreciate honesty. Most important, referees are less likely to mention limitations in reviews that you already have mentioned, unless the referees see them as fatal flaws.

Many authors nurse the hope that the referees will not notice the flaws. Such a hope is likely to be wishful thinking. Moreover, it is a misguided wish. Worse even than getting a paper rejected before publication is having to retract it after publication or having to resist an onslaught of published criticism for flaws that you should have noticed. Save yourself the trouble by acknowledging the flaws yourself.

12. *Write for your likely referees and readers.* Expert article writers do not just write articles. They write for an audience. They decide on likely journals before they put pen to paper (or fingers to computer keys).

You can get a good idea of the types of articles a given journal publishes simply by reading the journal's mission statement (usually near the front or back of the journal) and by looking at recent past issues. But there is a more informal kind of knowledge you need to acquire either through your own experience or by profiting from the experience of others.

Many characteristics of journals go beyond mission statements. Some journals seem to emphasize methodological rigor above all else. One reads them and has the feeling that the study could be infinitely trivial but nevertheless published as long as it was methodologically sound. Other journals seem to emphasize articles that are interesting but flakey: The ideas are provocative but the evidence for them is slim. Still other journals seem more concerned about length than about anything else. These journals will not publish relatively longer articles, no matter how good those articles may be. One journal to which I have submitted seems to care more that the article is in standard APA journal-article format than about what is said in this or any other format. These kinds of characteristics tend to come and go as the editorships of journals change, but oftentimes, the "culture" of a given journal endures beyond any single editorial board.

It thus behooves you to find out as much as you can about the kinds of issues that are important to the editor and referees of a given journal. You can save yourself a lot of lost time by seeking journals that publish the kind of article you have written and by avoiding journals that do not publish this kind of article.

Now that you have learned something about how to write your article with your referees in mind, do it. As for me, it is time for me to practice what I preach: I have to proofread my article.

Chapter 12

Reading Reviews, Suffering Rejection, and Advocating for Your Paper

MELISSA G. WARREN

If all you have ever received are letters accepting your paper for publication, you need not read this chapter. You are a member of a very small group; chances are its members would fit on the head of a pin. Most psychologists who write for publication, including those who are themselves editors, those whose names are well known, and those who seem to be able to place their papers everywhere, are the recipients of far more rejection letters than they have publications. For every paper that is published, there are likely to have been multiple submissions, most of them resulting in rejection. Next time you see a vita with 30 publications, you may correctly surmise that there are approximately 100 rejections letters behind it. How many rejection letters have you notched in your belt? If it is fewer than a dozen, you have only just begun.

To help keep your acceptance to rejection ratio within limits that are tolerable to you, there are small things you can do that will sometimes make a difference if a paper is straddling the line between a chance at publication and being sent home without a prize. These suggestions are based on the premise that the scholarly publishing process, like any other collective endeavor undertaken by humans, has developed its own informal but powerful norms and is guided not only by written rules, but by custom. Knowing the customs, or having tacit knowledge of the editorial process, gives one an advantage. Sternberg's research (Sternberg, Wagner, Williams, & Horvath, 1995) suggests that possession of tacit knowledge is what separates people who are great at their work from people who are

169

only good at it. Authors who understand what goes on behind the closed door of the editorial office will more often gain entry in large part because their behavior is consistent with the mores of the scholarly publishing culture.

Before discussing the culture and its mores, it is important to acknowledge that the process by which papers are selected for publication is flawed. Eloquent accounts of the perils of peer review, mean-spirited reviews, the errors and injustices perpetrated by editors, effects of concealing the identity of authors and reviewers, poor inter-rater reliability, and the irony of the imprecision and unscientific mien of the entire edifice appear regularly in the literature. The Comment section of the *American Psychologist*, for example, has long been one forum for expressions of discontent (Einhorn, 1971) and ideas about how we might do better (Epstein, 1995; Hunt, 1971; Newman, 1966; Rabinovich, 1996). Fortunately, empirical examinations of various aspects of the editorial process have been done since Fiske and Fogg (1990, 1993) lamented the dearth of data and published their study of the editorial practices of seven American Psychological Association (APA) published journals. Results of studies about peer review were published recently in two general medical journals (*JAMA* and *The New England Journal of Medicine*) and in the *British Journal of Psychiatry* (see Bibliography). It is hoped that a better system will develop as a result of the collective efforts of all the parties. Until there is a better way, authors who know the lay of the land are at an advantage.

GOODNESS OF FIT

Goodness of Fit is the #1 factor in successful submissions.[1] Send your paper to the journal that is most likely to smile on it. If your paper is on the same topic as most of the articles published in the *Journal of Your Dreams*, employs similar methodology, is comparable in length to what they typically publish, and is written in a clear and compati-

[1] This thought is not original to me. I heard it in graduate school from Harold Yuker, a pioneer in research on attitudes we hold toward disabilities and people who have them.

ble style, then it has a big jump on the other submissions. If it isn't a good fit with the previously published articles, then you probably sent it to the wrong journal.

There are over 600 journals in the field of psychology or fields closely related to it.[2] The advent of electronic databases for literature searches and inexpensive access to them was a great leveler. No longer must a paper appear in a big name journal or one with a large circulation in order to avoid oblivion. Papers that are useful will be found by the people who need them no matter where they originally appeared. There is no doubt that one's professional status depends in part on the status of the journals in which one has published, but that presumably is a secondary consideration to contributing to the litera ture so that others can benefit from the fruits of your scholarship. If the first priority is publishing a manuscript, do not send it to the journal that is most famous or boasts the highest rejection rate. Choose more thoughtfully than that. Look at many journals, select two or three that publish papers most similar to the one you wish to place, and submit it to the one you prefer. It is not permissible to submit a manuscript to more than one journal simultaneously for the simple reason that a journal invests time and money to handle submissions. Authors should abstain from engaging in this time-saving technique. Most journals operate on small budgets, so it is problematic for them to consider a paper that is later withdrawn. In addition to squander-ing their meager resources, it can imperil their production schedule. Editors are understandably annoyed by simultaneous submission of the same manuscript to different journals.

Some editors welcome preliminary communications from authors regarding goodness of fit (Fowler, 1993; Russ & Schenckman, 1980). Others do not. The area of the field covered and the resources avail-able to the editor are two features that probably have the most effect on how such inquiries are received. The *American Psychologist*, because it is a general journal with a full-time staff, encourages authors to write or call to discuss whether their paper is well suited for the journal. Editors of empirical journals whose mission is to

[2] *Journals in Psychology: A Resource Listing for Authors* (5th ed.) contains 355 titles, addresses, and statements of purpose and coverage statements of English language journals that publish papers by psychologists.

build the literature so that clearly articulated questions that are well
known to everyone in that area are answered as soon as possible may
be less amenable to hearing from authors. Talking to authors about
their paper's prospects is likely to be less important to them than
attending to papers that are going through the peer review process or
contributing to the knowledge base themselves. Another set of circumstances that should render an author cautious about contacting
an editor to ask about their paper's chances is the degree of importance played by methodology. If methodology is a big question in that
part of the field and one of the primary reasons that manuscripts are
rejected or accepted is the method of investigation chosen, the
answer to a query is likely to be, "Send me the paper, then we'll talk."
The editor will want to look at how you did what you did and see how
it holds up against their standards.

REACTIONS TO REJECTION

Presumably, you made certain that your paper was complete in
every respect before you sent it in and you spent hours polishing it
to a high shine. It was as perfect as you could make it. After sending
it off into the world, you wait to see what the editor and the reviewers say about it. To have your hopeful waiting room musings interrupted with the proclamation that your nearly perfect paper has
flaws by the dozen is painful no matter how seasoned, sophisticated, or senior the author. When you are the recipient of an unexpected rejection letter, don't sit down and fire off a letter to the
editor. Talk it over with your friends. Indulge in intemperate verbal
expressions to your colleagues. Write a letter to the editor that says
exactly what you want to say, then delete it.

Once emotional reactions have subsided, and before sending an
irate letter to the editor, the wise author looks at the reviews to see if
they contain anything of value. Authors who are savvy readers of
reviews and decision letters have an edge over those who aren't. This
chapter, written from the perspective of an editor, provides tacit
knowledge about how some editors think about their editorial work
and offers suggestions for authors who are dissatisfied with the
reviews they get and/or the use the editor made of the reviews.

Reviewers come in all varieties, like the pool of people from which they are drawn. Some reviewers are overly critical and seem to view the opportunity to offer anonymous comments as one in which to indulge in more extreme behavior. There are generous reviewers who will spend two hours generating a careful critique and offering many suggestions about how the paper could be strengthened. Conscientiousness varies widely, as does time on task. On rare occasions, a reviewer will be struck in a personal way by a manuscript and respond to it with vehemence. Editors know that reviewers and reviews run the gamut. They take that into consideration when they read the reviews. Reviews are weighted differently depending in part on who wrote them, known biases they hold, their areas of expertise, their proximity to the author or the work done by the author, their typical manner of reviewing manuscripts, private asides to the editor, and sometimes qualifiers stated explicitly in the review. Editors base their decisions on the reviews but they are not bound by them. The types of decisions editors make, the ways in which some of them weight reviews, and when authors can expect their paper to undergo a second round of peer review are described in a later section (Categories of Editorial Decisions), after a brief introduction to Fiske and Fogg's entertaining and informative tutorial on how to read reviews, below.

HOW TO THINK ABOUT REVIEWS

"But the Reviewers are Making Different Criticisms of My Paper!" is the title of an article on this topic that appeared in the *American Psychologist*. Fiske and Fogg (1990) did a study of 153 papers and the 402 reviews the papers elicited. Then they wrote a very good article about their findings and published a brief follow-up 3 years later about how the editors in their sample used reviews (Fiske & Fogg, 1993). Reviewers *will* say different things about the same manuscript. Authors should not look for consistency or complain to the editor that the reviewers are contradicting one another. That is to be expected, it is sometimes even by design. Remember convergent validity? Multimatrix multimodal methods? Bear those in mind when reading reviews and decision letters. The perspectives of your target audience will vary at least as much as those of the reviewers. Your goal, presumably, is to reach as many colleagues as possible with your message, so use the range of opinions expressed by the reviewers to help you put something for everyone in your paper.

One of the most interesting findings of Fiske and Fogg's excellent analysis of reviews is that fully 65% of their critical comments are directed at *how* the author presented his or her work. The remaining criticisms were about things that are usually immutable after a study has been completed, such as methodological issues and the rationale for carrying it out in the first place. This means that the quality of your work is not necessarily the decisive factor in whether it reaches publication. How you present your work in writing is probably just as important. Clarity and completeness of explication are essential, as is following the rules. Report everything that the APA's *Publication Manual* (1994) says should be reported. Don't follow the examples of other authors. Myriad count and sort studies of the literature itself have repeatedly shown that most of what is published is deficient in important ways. Draw the tables and figures according to the specifications in the *Publication Manual*. Be meticulous about following the rules, all the rules, not just the ones you remember. Many reviews point out omissions, lack of specificity, lack of clarity, inadequate description of scoring or measures used, and missing results. Avoid these preventable negative evaluations by being thorough.

Fiske and Fogg (1990) catalogued and categorized 3,477 criticisms contained in 402 reviews.[3] Authors can benefit from their work in numerous ways. They made a table showing types of criticisms and gave the particular criticisms of that type that are made. For example, one category of criticisms that are made of Results sections is planning and execution; a particular criticism of the planning and execution is that the results are puzzling or difficult to interpret. A paper that has been scrutinized in light of Fiske and Fogg's classification of criticisms, either by its author or an informal reviewer, will stand a better chance of surviving peer review.

---

[3] Susan Fiske, a graduate student at that time, now a renowned psychologist, did most of the scut work required to count and sort the comments made by the reviewers. Donald Fiske and his coauthor, Louis Fogg, are the authors of the article.

Get your own reviews first. Don't send your paper into hostile territory without first having it vetted by friendly readers. Friends and colleagues will find imperfections in what you thought was a perfect paper. Fiske and Fogg's (1990) sagacity is revealed in their recommendation that you show your paper to an enemy if you want even more useful feedback. People who like you or who want you to favor them will rarely assume the burden of telling you when your paper is way off the mark. They more often encourage you to send it to the top journal in the area because they want to encourage you and they know that there are many others willing to deliver bad news. An adversarial review, on the other hand, will give you information you can use to strengthen your paper, as well as a more realistic idea of what its reception in the world of scholarly publishing will be like. Follow Fiske and Fogg's advice to cultivate an enemy with whom you can exchange papers. Even if you are in the unfortunate position of not having an enemy and friendly reviews are the only kind you can get, don't let your paper leave home without them. Just bear in mind that your friends are probably apt to tend to your emotional well-being rather than providing rigorous criticism.

CATEGORIES OF EDITORIAL DECISIONS

Editorial decisions fall into five categories: (a) accept; (b) reject without peer review; (c) reject with peer review; (d) revise and resubmit; and (e) revise and resubmit, but not to this journal. These categories are not as cut and dried as they appear. There are subtypes of revise and resubmit. Editors differ in the names they give to these categories, and the same decision may mean different things to different editors. Over the years, purposeful discussions of editors who have edited journals published by APA[4] have illuminated myriad individual differences in the types of decisions used, the frequency with which editors' decisions fall into various categories, and what editors mean when they instruct authors in what revisions

---

[4] Readers should bear in mind that APA only publishes a couple dozen journals, which is a tiny proportion of the pool.

to make. Those discussions have not led to more consistency across editors. Rather, they underscore the importance of authors being aware of the particulars of the situation at hand and the importance of gathering as much information as possible about the editorial practices of the journal of interest.

Accept

Editors rarely accept a manuscript for publication as submitted. The reason for this probably has something to do with the need all people have to distinguish themselves from others by showing that they have refined taste, or a discriminating palate, or some other faculty that makes them who they are.

Rejection without Review

Manuscripts are rejected without peer review when the editor is certain that they would not survive because they fall outside the scope of the journal's purview or they are flawed in a way that would require an inordinate amount of time and effort to correct. The proportion of manuscripts rejected without review ranges from 0 to 70%. There are few data regarding rejection without review. My sense of what transpires is based on conversations with and among editors and my own experience. Some editors do not read manuscripts before sending them out. This practice is based on the belief that every author is entitled to receive feedback from colleagues. Other editors, primarily those who edit journals that publish the results of research in a well-defined area of the field studied by a relatively small, highly specialized group of researchers, report that all the submissions they receive are a good fit and 100% of their submissions are sent out for review. The *American Psychologist* rejects about 75% of all submissions without review. The high rate is due to many factors. Because it is a general journal, papers from every area of the field are candidates. This stands in marked contrast to journals devoted to a particular part of the field with a corresponding reduction in the pool of authors who might reasonably submit manuscripts. Second, because it is widely distributed, the *American Psychologist* is one journal that readily comes to mind when authors contemplate possible outlets for their work. Third, authors seem to like to get their papers into journals with large circulations, although, as discussed in the section Goodness of Fit, the accessibility of scholarly information via electronic sources undermines the argument about dissemination, leaving this preference resting on employment and tenure. Other contributing factors to high rates of rejection without review at some general journals are the difficulty of writing for a general audience, the lack of broad appeal of some specialties no matter how well they are presented, and the prohibition against empirical papers.

Many authors do not make the leap from highly technical language, because it is customary and perhaps necessary when communicating with colleagues in their areas of specialty, to a style that is accessible to all psychologists regardless of their areas of specialty. Regarding the relevance of specialties to the whole, there is no doubt that all are important. Specialties developed in response to our need to discover more about the world. Some specialties are of broader appeal than others because they touch more people, and more psychologists, directly. For example, everyone feels entitled to an opinion about child rearing practices but few people wonder about the neural bases of how children learn to use language. The same principle holds true in psychology. There are topics about which all psychologists should possess specialized knowledge, but the list of topics does not include all areas of the field.

Rejection after Review

A typical rejection letter informs the author that reviews were obtained from one or more reviewers and that the paper is not accepted for publication in the journal. Reviews are enclosed and the author is urged to look elsewhere for acceptance. This type of rejection is definitive and final. Nothing is to be gained by revising and resubmitting to that journal. Time spent doing so is time lost. The realistic author will take what the reviews offer that is helpful, select a different journal, and rewrite the paper to fit that journal. Most editors will not reconsider a paper that was rejected. Their rationale is that they spent the money and did the job once. Doing it a second time constitutes squandering resources because a second round of reviews will result in the same outcome. If they see any prospect of publishing a revised version of the paper, the author will be invited to revise and resubmit.

Revise and Resubmit

From both an author's and the editor's perspective, this is the most desirable category. The letter of decision from the editor reports that reviews were obtained and that if the author revises the paper in the prescribed manner, it stands a good chance of being accepted for publication. The author may wonder, "How good is a good chance?" It depends. Depending on the extent of the revisions, the vehemence and the identity of the reviewers, the familiarity of the editor with the areas of the field covered by the paper, and the disposition of the editor, a good chance may mean 99% or it may mean 50%. Given the rejection rates of many journals, a 50% chance is markedly higher than where the paper began. It is my impression that editors do not invite an author to revise and resubmit if the manuscript's chances of publication in the journal are less than 50–50. In the absence of data, these proportions reflect rules of thumb derived from my sense of how editors do their job.

Authors may wonder whether their revised manuscript will go through a second round of peer review or if the editor will decide its fate. Some editors tell authors what procedure they will use, conveying the information in the decision letter. Others don't. Some editors have a rule they apply in every situation; others play it by ear. If the question of whether to obtain more reviews is decided on a case by case basis, the same variables that influence the manuscript's chances of publication are operational. If an editor knows the area well and the reviewers' suggestions were fairly easy to implement, the likelihood that a second round of reviews are needed is low. If the editor isn't expert in the topics covered by the paper, the reviewers were vehement and the criticisms far ranging, and there is ample room for interpretation in how the revisions were made, the likelihood of further review is higher.

Authors may reasonably inquire as to the editor's plan for the revised manuscript. It may be helpful to know whether reviews will be solicited, whether the same reviewers or new ones will be used, or whether the editor will make a decision without further review. Authors should bear in mind that there is no single right method of handling a manuscript that was revised and resubmitted at the invitation of the editor. Some editors have a policy of only showing the paper to the same reviewers who saw the first version on the grounds that to solicit new reviews constitutes double jeopardy. Some editors use all new reviewers because they believe they know what the first group would say and they want the paper to have the benefit of a fresh look. Some editors use a combination of first round reviewers and new reviewers. From the author's perspective, the invitation to revise and resubmit offers a good opportunity to learn more about what the editor desires in a paper and the procedures the editor follows, and to advocate for the paper. Simply calling or writing the editor to ask about the procedure he or she intends to follow can be an occasion for a cordial and informative exchange. Rely on the standard human courtesies to advance your cause. It is a safe bet to assume that any editor would prefer to go through a revision and its attendant exchanges in a collegial manner rather than in a combative one. As discussed in a following section (Advocating for Your Paper), the cover letter that accompanies the revised version is a very important component of effective advocacy.

Revise but Don't Resubmit

A decision letter that describes the revisions an author should make but does not extend an invitation to resubmit the manuscript is a rejection. Authors should think of it as a friendly rejection. It is probably a subcategory, but for some journals, a fairly large proportion of manuscripts reach this outcome, which makes it an important category for authors to consider.

As a rule, an editor will take the time to deviate from writing a standard rejection letter if the paper of the reviews elicit his or her interest. If the editor believes the paper could be published elsewhere and wants to take the time to tell the author how it might be improved prior to submission elsewhere, the letter might describe in detail revisions that seem likely to result in eventual publication. Similarly, if the reviews seem representative of the kind of feedback the paper will elicit again, suggestions for revision may be offered.

Authors should not misinterpret the editor's suggestions for revision or encouragement regarding future publication as an implicit invitation to resubmit to the same journal. If the suggestions or encouragement truly are helpful and the author feels so inclined, a thank you might be in order. When the paper is published elsewhere, it may be a good idea to send a reprint to the editor who rejected it but offered help or encouragement. Only authors with good social skills and mastery of the graceful written note, or those with a sense of the nonspecific factors involved are advised to do this. The pitfall is that the reprint could be perceived as the equivalent of saying, "Nah-Nah" or, more eloquently, "At least some editors can recognize a good paper when they see one." If those are your sentiments, it is best to abstain from sending a reprint or otherwise informing the editor of your happy occasion.

ADVOCATING FOR YOUR PAPER

First and foremost, before contacting the editor, read the coverage statement of the journal and all previous editorials by the current editor. The editor is talking to you in those pieces, and if you weren't listening, you may have missed some important assumptions, be unaware of certain practices, or have unrealistic expectations. When you approach an editor, it is within the context of those prior communications, whether you know what they were or not. The editor's position may make more sense if you know the context. Coverage statements are carefully drafted paragraphs that often appear in each issue of the journal. They are usually developed with all of the journals in a given subfield in mind. Generally, publishers and editors try to carve out a niche for a journal and to avoid unnecessary competition with others that cover the same area. This is not to say competition between journals is rare. Given the large number of journals in psychology, most specialties have several journals that publish similar kinds of papers. But some journals become known as particularly hospitable to certain kinds of work, by design, happenstance, or a combination of both, and their coverage statements may reflect those affinities. Editors may agree among themselves to divvy up the area and will inform readers in coverage statements and editorials. The first editorial of an editor, published at the outset of his or her term as editor, is a good place to look for clues about whether your paper is a good fit, or why it was rejected.

Don't argue specifics. Authors who hope to change the editor's mind, either about a particular decision or about what is important for the field, sometimes go about it by offering a persuasive, point by point refutation of a review or point of view expressed or implied by the editor. In my opinion, this is not a good tactical decision. First, it assumes that the editor's decision or mind is mutable, which may be a false assumption. Second, reviews are not usually written to stand up to a point–counterpoint style of arguing. Reviewers don't usually offer support for their conclusions. The typical communication from a reviewer is intended to advise the editor of his or her thoughts about the manuscript and the approach it brings to bear on a problem. Third, it can have the effect of putting the editor on the defensive. What options are left to the editor beyond either the forced choice to enter into the point–counterpoint exchange and defend the reviews as a sound basis for decision, or to simply issue a terse affirmation of the decision? Very few. They might obtain an additional review, and that will occasionally lead to a reconsideration of the decision. If that is what is desired, authors would be better advised to ask for it directly than to dispute the content of the reviews that accompanied the decision letter.

A corollary to the prohibition against arguing specifics is, "Don't argue that the reviews were weighted wrongly," or that there were enough positive reviews to lead to a favorable decision rather than a negative one. The editors I know never tire of saying, "Editors aren't vote counters." I think they say it a lot because a common complaint they hear from authors is that the reviews were split so their manuscripts should get the benefit of the doubt, or that two reviewers liked it and only one didn't, so the decision should be to accept the paper. In the vast majority of submissions, editors have their own opinions about the paper and aren't completely reliant on the judgment of the reviewers. Unlike the reviewers, they are considering not only the merits of the manuscript, but its fit with the journal, its relation to other work by the author, and its place in the literature. A third reason that editors don't abide by a "majority rules" dictum is that reviews may be assigned different weights, as discussed above.

If you don't argue specifics or dispute the editor's reading of the reviews, how can you advocate for your paper? Up front, in the cover letter that accompanies the manuscript and again in the first page of the paper itself, make a strong case for why this particular topic is important at this point in time. Paint a vivid picture of the gap in the literature it spans, or the recent, highly publicized phenomenon it explains, or identify and explain the need others in the field have for this paper. Do this in two or three sentences at most. Just as journalists persuade readers of the importance of any given article by the use of a hook, authors of scholarly papers must focus the reader, or editor's attention, on the raison d'etre for the existence of this manuscript.

Second, if there is any doubt that the editor is familiar with the niche that the paper is written to fill, enclose relevant materials and summarize them in a sentence or two in the cover letter. Reprints of works by the author that contain an exhortation for someone to address the topic are less convincing than recent works by recognized voices of authority in that area. Establishing the credentials or prior publications of the author is not necessary. The content and utility of the paper itself are much more important than the qualifications of the author.

Third, in the event of a rejection, write a letter telling why you disagree with the decision but stop short of saying it should be overturned. Show it to four colleagues and ask them to put themselves in the place of the editor who is slated to receive it. Ask how it would sound to them if they were the editor. Try to strike a balance between forceful expression and an undertone of anger. Pose thoughtful questions rather than demanding answers. For example, if you believe the editor has overlooked the importance of the approach you took in the manuscript, rather than writing something along the lines of, "How could you underestimate the importance of Mueller's work given the questions memory researchers currently face?" try, "Do you know of any approaches that can shed light on the main questions in current memory research and skirt Mueller's work?" Maybe the editor, prompted by your question, will rethink the matter, or maybe you will get an answer that will help you reformulate your approach. A reasoned, low-key letter is more likely to elicit a good response from anyone, even an editor, than is a highly emotional and accusing one.

REFUSE TO REVISE

There are occasions when an author should not comply with requests to revise, even if compliance with the instructions is a guarantee of publication in the journal one most desired. If the revisions recommended would undermine the main message of the paper or distort the author's intent to the degree that the paper would stand in contrast to his or her body of work, *don't do it.* A third reason to refuse to incorporate the requested revisions is if the review(s) are based on a different system of evaluation or premised on assumptions that are so disparate that the revised paper could not span the two frames of reference and remain internally consistent.

Editors are aware of and concerned about, in greater and lesser degrees, the variables in scholarly publishing that interact in unintended ways and produce papers that please everyone, and hence please no one. The pitfalls of committee authored papers are well known, and a much revised article can approach the boundaries of the territory occupied by committee reports. Editors vary among themselves, and individual editors may well vary over time, in where they locate the point of equilibrium between letting authors present their contribution in the most compelling manner versus requiring revisions designed to bring the paper into conformity with the scientific ideals of standing on the shoulders of those who came before, adhering to current methodological and statistical norms, giving opposing positions due consideration, and presenting one's findings and conclusions objectively. When the editor doesn't find the balance between preserving the author's message and incorporating the suggestions of the reviewers, the author must persuade the editor to follow a different course or withdraw the paper and submit it elsewhere. It is easier to resist recommendations for revision and redirect one's paper when one is not feeling pressed by the demands associated with employment or grant applications. If one can exercise the choice to withdraw even in the face of an offer of publication, the realm of available choices becomes a little bit wider, which may bring concomitant positive feelings. Feelings aside, if a paper made it to the point of being accepted contingent on revisions at one journal, its chances of success at another journal are fairly good.

When an author decides not to revise and resubmit, a letter informing the editor is not only courteous but standard practice. In the interest of advocacy, the author might explain the rationale for the decision and tell the editor of the intent to submit elsewhere. An eloquent letter that has drawn on all available sources of information, and been scrutinized by careful readers for clarity, substantive content, and emotional tone, is most likely to enhance your prospects of publishing in that journal or under the auspices of that editor in the future. An announcement of your intent, rather than one that leaves the ball in the editor's court or demands a response that will inform your next step, is the best type to send.

CONCLUSION

Even if you feel as if you are Alice attending the Mad Tea Party, remember that you came of your own accord and on occasion remind yourself that unlike Alice, you know the way out. If you elect to stay, develop a cordial acquaintance with the editor whenever you are dealing with one that is amenable to it. Keep in touch with the editor by letter or e-mail at regular intervals but without applying pressure for a quicker or favorable decision. Let the editor know whether you are willing to modify the paper if asked to do so. Demonstrate that you understand the rules and customs and have no intention of burdening him or her with frequent or unpleasant demands for information or explanation. Offer to provide the names of prospective reviewers if that would be welcome and offer to serve as a reviewer in the future should the need arise. Finally, accept rejection gracefully if it comes. Always keep two or three journals in mind whose mission and coverage fits with your work. Try again next time you have a paper that seems to be a good fit with that journal.

REFERENCES

American Psychological Association (1994). *Publication Manual of the American Psychological Association* (4th ed.). Washington, DC: Author.

Bedeian, A. G. (1996). Improving the journal review process: The question of ghostwriting. *American Psychologist, 51,* 1189.

Brysbaert, M. (1996). Improving the journal review process and the risk of making the poor poorer. *American Psychologist, 51,* 1193.

Epstein, S. (1995). What can be done to improve the journal review process. *American Psychologist, 50,* 883–885.

Fine, M. A. (1996). Reflections on enhancing accountability in the peer review process. *American Psychologist, 51,* 1190–1191.

Fiske, D. W., & Fogg, L. (1990). But the reviewers are making different cricitisms of my paper! Diversity and uniqueness in reviewer comments. *American Psychologist, 45,* 591–598.

Fogg, L., & Fiske, D. W. (1993). Foretelling the judgments of reviewers and editors. *American Psychologist, 48,* 293–294.

Fowler, R. D. (1993). Statement of editorial policy: 1993. *American Psychologist, 48,* 5–7.

Hunt, E. (1971). Psychological publications. *American Psychologist, 26,* 311.

Levenson, R. L. (1996). Enhance the journals, not the review process. *American Psychologist, 51,* 1191–1192.

Newman, S. H. (1966). Improving the evaluation of submitted manuscripts. *American Psychologist, 21,* 980–981.

Rabinovich, B. A. (1996). A perspective on the journal review process. *American Psychologist, 51,* 1190.

Russ, R. C., & Schenckman, R. I. (1980). Editorial statement: Theory and method and their basis in psychological investigation. *Journal of Mind & Behavior, 1,* 1–7.

BIBLIOGRAPHY

Bornstein, R. F. (1994). Costs and benefits of reviewer anonymity: A survey of journal editors and manuscript reviewers. *Journal of Social Behavior & Personality, 8,* 355–370.

Crammer, J. L. (1998). Editor creates journal. *British Journal of Psychiatry, 173,* 114.

Crandall, R. (1977). How qualified are the editors? *American Psychologist, 32,* 578–579.

Einhorn, H. (1971). Responsibility of journal editors and referees. *American Psychologist, 26,* 600–601.

Epstein, S. (1995). What can be done to improve the journal review process. *American Psychologist, 50,* 883.

Gilbert, J. R., Williams, E. S., & Lundberg, G. D. (1995). Is there gender bias in JAMA's peer review process? *Journal of the American Medical Association, 272,* 139–142.

Gilliland, S. W., & Cortina, J. M. (1997). Reviewer and editor decision making in the journal review process. *Personnel Psychology, 50,* 427–452.

Godlee, F., Gale, C. R., & Martyn, C. N. (1998). Effect on the quality of peer review of blinding reviewers and asking them to sign their reports: A randomized control trial. *Journal of the American Medical Association, 280,* 237–240.

Gottfredson, S. D. (1979). Evaluating psychological research reports: Dimensions, reliability, and correlates of quality judgments. *American Psychologist, 33,* 920–934.

Howard, L., & Wilkinson, G. (1998). Peer review and editorial decision-making. *British Journal of Psychiatry, 173,* 110–113.

Hunt, E. (1971). Psychological publications. *American Psychologist, 26,* 311.

Justice, A. C., Cho, M. K., Winker, M. A. Berlin, J. A., & Rennie, D. (1998). Does masking author identity improve peer review quality? A randomized controlled trial. *Journal of the American Medical Association, 280,* 240–242.

Lindsey, D. (1976). Distinction, achievement, and editorial board membership. *American Psychologist, 31,* 799–804.

Lykken, D. T. (1974). Time for Cerberus to give his name. *American Psychologist, 29,* 64.

Matocha, L. (1993). Do editors have obligations to authors? *Marriage & Family Review, 18,* 31–39.

Newman, S. (1966). lmproving the evaluation of submitted manuscripts. *American Psychologist, 21,* 980–981.

Rabinovich, B. (1996). A perspective on the journal review process. *American Psychologist, 51,* 1190.

Roediger, H. L. (1987). The role of journal editors in the scientific process. In D. N. Jackson & J. P. Rushton (Eds.), *Scientific excellence: Origins and assessment.* Newbury Park, CA: Sage.

Rogoff, B. (1998). Behind the scenes: Observations of the editorial process. *Human Development, 41,* 1–6.

Stacey, B. G. (1993). The uses of psychology journals. *The Psychologist: Bulletin of the British Psychological Society, 6,* 12–15.

Sternberg, R., Wagner, R., Williams, W., & Horveth, J. (1995). Testing common sense. *American Psychologist, 50,* 912–927.

Susser, M. B. (1994). The Charybdis of publishing in academia. *Marriage & Family Review, 18,* 161–169.

van Rooyen, S., Godlee, F., Evans, S., Smith, R., & Black, N. (1998). Effect of blinding and unmasking on the quality of peer review: A randomized trial. *Journal of the American Medical Association, 280,* 234–237.

Watkins, M. W. (1979). Chance and interrater agreement on manuscripts. *American Psychologist, 34,* 796–798.

Wolff, W. M. (1974). Publication problems in psychology and an explicit evaluation schema for manuscripts. *American Psychologist, 28,* 257–261.

Chapter 13

Rewriting the Psychology Paper

RICHARD K. WAGNER

Two days ago I had a weekly meeting with a graduate student who is among my best students ever. She had arrived with a Master's degree in hand, and in short order, she wrote a review paper, an empirical article that is about to be sent off for possible publication, and has defended her dissertation prospectus. The agenda for our meeting was to consider predictions made by alternative models that she would evaluate for her dissertation.

Meetings with productive graduate students are the meetings faculty most look forward to, and this was no exception. Before talking about her proposed dissertation, however, the student stated that she had heard from a journal. It took me a second to remember that she had sent her review paper to a journal about 4 months ago. This was the first article she had written for a psychology-related journal, and would be her first sole-authored publication if accepted.

Unfortunately, the news was that her article had been rejected. She handed me the letter from the editor and the sole review. The editor thanked her for sending the manuscript to the journal, and wished her well in revising the article for possible publication elsewhere. I turned to the review. It began in a begrudging, complimentary fashion, noting that the writing was "pretty good" and that the conceptual views reviewed in the manuscript were "interesting." In the course of my university career, I've read several thousand reviews, either as part of the review process for someone else's work or for my own. Although one can try to read between the lines too much, I sensed tension, as though the reviewer were angry about something.

I wondered what the problem had been. The article wasn't overly long – something that does tax reviewers who have many demands on their time. The article wasn't critical in the sense of challenging or attacking someone's work or cherished position, so it didn't seem possible that we had offended someone. Although the point of the article was to bring material from other disciplines into a discipline that had not yet made these connections, the article seemed to be within the realm of what the journal purported to publish. So we shouldn't have been wasting the reviewer's time with a manuscript that was a bad fit to the journal. The writing really was good, in terms of clarity, so the reviewer should not have become frustrated trying to figure out what my student intended to communicate.

Then I came across the sentences that made clear what the problem was. The reviewer commented on a conceptual problem, namely, that the manuscript had not included a view the reviewer believed to be relevant to the discussion. The reviewer pointed us to a book. My heart sank when I reviewed the editorial board of the journal and realized that the author of the book was the likely reviewer of my student's manuscript.

Although we don't know that what the outcome might have been otherwise, we certainly hurt our chances seriously by not citing potentially relevant work done by the reviewer. What made this lesson even more painful was my memory of sending off my first manuscript from graduate school. After a number of revisions, my advisor agreed that we were ready to send off the manuscript and asked me to get the guidelines to authors and editorial board composition of the journal we had selected. When we next met, he reviewed the composition of the editorial board looking for individuals whose work we should have cited but had not. If I had done this same exercise with my graduate student, the outcome might have been more positive. To add insult to injury, the topic of my dissertation (Wagner, 1987), and some other work I have done (Sternberg et al., 2000; Sternberg & Wagner, 1986; Wagner & Sternberg, 1985, 1987) was the importance of tacit knowledge (i.e., practical know-how that usually is not taught formally) to professional achievement in domains including academic psychology. My dissertation established that tacit knowledge about the ins and outs of publishing was related to outcome criteria, including number of publications and citation count. Had I learned nothing from my dissertation and from the wisdom of my helpful advisor?

I don't purport to have any special wisdom about publishing, which won't be much of a surprise, given the experience I just related about my graduate student's first psychology manuscript. It also is the case that excellent guidance on scientific writing exists (e.g., Sternberg, 1993). I do think some practical information about publishing, such as avoid slighting an individual by not citing his or her work when you should have, rarely gets discussed. Perhaps the best example of such an omission is the topic of rewriting. Virtually no manuscript is accepted in original form. But in my experience, skillful rewriting – revising one's manuscript in response to feedback from editors, reviewers, colleagues, or even your own initial reading – is not fully appreciated.

BEING MISERLY WITH WORDS BUT NOT WITH CITATIONS

Most drafts of manuscripts need a good bit of pruning. When writing for publication, economy counts. Every word must serve a purpose. Page limitations preclude irrelevant material. But although it is vital to be economical in choice of words and content, one nevertheless should be generous in attempting to relate one's own ideas to those of others.

When my advisor scanned the editorial board to see if we omitted relevant citations of potential reviewers, I thought it to be a rather cynical enterprise. After all, if someone's work had not surfaced when I was writing the Introduction or Discussion, why stick it in now – besides the self-serving answer of wanting to improve my chances of having the manuscript accepted for publication? My reaction reflected two assumptions that I now believe to be naïve if not erroneous.

The first assumption was that the identity of all related work would be known in the routine course of carrying out my research. Given the sheer volume of what is published annually, it is likely that an author will be unaware of relevant work of at least someone. Fortunately, having the bad luck of having one's work reviewed by that someone is a bit rarer. In the case of my graduate student, her area is an active one, with a large number of books and relevant articles. In our defense, the book we missed was not particularly recent or notable. But it was an omission. Most writers, including myself, tend to overvalue the contribution of their own ideas and writing, and undervalue those of others. This bias, combined with the practical difficulty of keeping abreast of exploding literatures, makes it probable that one will omit potentially relevant work. Scanning the editorial boards of all of the journals in an area, as well as study section rosters for grant funding agencies, is one way to identify possible omissions because these individuals tend to be among the major contributors to their areas of expertise.

My second erroneous assumption was that reviewers would approach, if not actually achieve, complete objectivity in their appraisal of one's manuscript. By its very nature, writing a review represents a combination of subjective and objective elements. As a reviewer, when I read a manuscript that I perceive to be closely related to a contribution of someone else, and that contribution is not cited, it is hard for me not to infer that the author is a little arrogant, ignorant, or careless. What we know about human judgment and decision making suggests it is likely that evaluation of a manuscript is colored by such inferences. I believe that we conveyed one or more of these impressions to the reviewer of my graduate student's manuscript, none of which bodes well for a positive outcome.

In retrospect, my changing view about the value of generously citing the work of others was predicted by results from my dissertation (Wagner, 1987). I asked academic psychologists, graduate students, and undergraduate students to rate the quality of various research-related strategies on two scales. An *ideal* scale represented the value of the strategy ideally, without regard to practical reality. An *actual* scale represented the practical value of the various strategies, given the world of academic psychology as it exists. The interesting finding was that discrepancies between ideal and actual ratings decreased with experience, being largest for undergraduates, next largest for graduate students, and virtually nil for experienced academic psychologists. Whether the convergence of actual and ideal noted for experienced academic psychologists represented (a) slippage in their ideals over time, (b) a selection factor, in that individuals whose ideals were closer to realities were more likely to select and stay in a profession, or (c) both, wasn't clear and still isn't. I now believe that generously citing the work of others is an important correction for a natural egocentrism that is common among writers, and fortuitously reduces the probability of offending reviewers who feel slighted by our omitting reference to their work.

SOLICITING FEEDBACK ACTIVELY

Part of the process of writing for publication is receiving feedback from reviewers and editors. But the amount of feedback obtained can be variable, and in general, is paltry relative to the feedback available to those who seek it actively.

With the exception of the occasional sadistic reviewer, most of us find it more pleasant and easier to give positive feedback than negative. Consequently, negative feedback may be left unstated. But with some diligence and tact, it often is possible to obtain negative feedback.

Most colleagues and mentors are quite willing to be a source of additional feedback. Individuals are flattered that you value their judgment enough to ask them to provide comments on a manuscript. By explicitly asking for suggestions about how to make the manuscript better, you provide individuals with a comfortable way to convey negatives in a constructive way.

The obvious consequence of actively seeking feedback is an increase in the amount of feedback you get. Because not all feedback is valid, an increase in the amount of feedback you obtain means an increase in invalid as well as valid feedback.

SEPARATING THE WHEAT FROM THE CHAFF

Feedback needs to be evaluated rather than accepted at face value. Reviews typically contain some good advice and some not-so-good advice. Given the amount of time you have spent on your project, and the comparably minimal time a reviewer spends, it is not surprising that some feedback will be unwise or simply wrong.

Beyond this, it is important to determine, as best one can, whether the editor and/or reviewers want a successful outcome for you, or whether they are convinced that your manuscript is a poor fit to the journal and their views are not likely to change regardless of revision. Ideally, but not always, the editor's intentions will be clearly spelled out in the action letter that accompanies the reviews. If the overall impression of the editor or reviewer is positive, he or she may try to provide recommendations and comments for revision in a genuine attempt to improve the final product. On the other hand, the editor or reviewer may believe that the topic of the manuscript simply is not interesting enough to merit publication, given the existing literature. But many editors and reviewers are not comfortable condemning a manuscript outright for something that cannot be fixed. So rather than doing so, they provide a laundry list of more specific comments and recommendations. They attempt to justify the global decision with specific comments and recommendations that really are chaff, as in the strips of metal foil released in the atmosphere to inhibit radar, as opposed to feedback that, if implemented, would result in acceptance of the manuscript.

PERSEVERANCE

Despite the fact that publishing is one of the two principal ways that psychologists influence their respective fields (the other is influencing students who subsequently publish), why do so many reduce their rate of publishing – if not stop entirely – when tenure or promotion no longer are at stake? The answer in part may be the low rate of return for their effort, as well as the unpleasantness of the process of peer review. Most manuscripts are rejected for publication by the selective, valued journals in a given field. Rejection rates for APA journals, for example, typically are 80% or higher. Of the smaller proportion of manuscripts that are eventually published, few will have an impact, as measured by citation count – the frequency with which the article is cited by someone else who publishes an article, chapter, or book. In fact, the citation counts of the majority of scientists in any field including psychology are near 0. This means that in a typical year, someone who succeeds in publishing will not make reference to any publication of the typical researcher.

Nevertheless, a small proportion of individuals will have a profound effect on a field. The distribution of citation counts is highly skewed. Although the majority of scientists have citation rates near 0, a minority have citation rates in excess of 100. In most fields that have been studied, the top 10% of most prolific contributors account for roughly half of everything produced, and the top 20% account for roughly 80% of everything produced (Simonton, 1996).

Dennis (1955), for example, studied the distribution of productivity in seven fields: eighteenth-century American secular music; books in Library of Congress as of 1942; publications in the fields of gerontology and geriatrics; publications in the field of North American geology from 1929–1939; publications on infantile paralysis to 1944; entries in *Chemical Abstracts* from 1937–1947, and publications on linguistics from 1939–1947. The combined results were that the top 10% of producers contributed 50% of the work. For publications in the field of psychology, the top 10% of producers contributed 40% of work, while the bottom 50% contributed only 15% of work (Dennis, 1954).

What is it that differentiates the top producers from the rest of the pack? One possibility is that they simply have more success publishing their work. In other words, their "hit rate" is higher because the quality of what they produce is higher. Early studies that examined ratios of contribution quality (i.e., those that had a measurable impact) to quantity (total number of contributions) suggested that this might indeed be the case (Dennis, 1966). However, these analyses were flawed in comparing quality of contributions from one database to total number of contributions in another (Simonton, 1988). When more recent studies compared quality and quantity of contributions for the same producers, a different pattern of results emerged (Simonton, 1985). This pattern of results is well described by the equal-odds rule, which holds that there is a relatively constant proportion of quality to quantity of contributions across individual researchers and within individual researchers across different time periods in their career. What differentiates top producers from the rest of the pack is not a higher hit rate, but sheer productivity. They surpass others in hits or quality contributions, but also in total contributions that include misses.

REACTING ADAPTIVELY

Negative feedback is directed at our manuscripts rather than ourselves. Most guidelines that editors send to reviewers make clear that *ad hominem* attacks are inappropriate, and conscientious editors interdict any such comments rather than send them on to authors. Nevertheless, it is hard not to take negative comments and decisions about one's manuscripts personally. The temptation is to counterattack, especially if there were inaccuracies in reviewers' comments, as is likely to be the case.

The first thing to do is to find a way to handle your anger and disappointment in a way that does not jeopardize what you are trying to accomplish. Early in my career I found hanging three fake voodoo dolls on my office door, labeled editor, reviewer 1, and reviewer 2, as well as venting with my colleagues, to be effective in dissipating anger. Disappointment had been harder for me. I remember having my Master's thesis rejected by a premier journal in my area. I believe I got the letter on Friday, and recall taking a ride on my bicycle the following day and thinking, over and over, that "this was big," that it "would have consequences on my job prospects." I never found a way to short-circuit disappointment the way that the voodoo dolls short-circuited anger. The only solutions were time to get over it and having other projects to attend to.

A mistake I see colleagues make that I believe arises from anger is engaging in pointless debates with editors that, at best, will win intellectual points but won't affect the outcome for the manuscript. The editors to engage are those whose letters encourage revising and resubmitting. When given the opportunity to revise and resubmit, the effective strategy is to deal with every point in the letter from the editor and each reviewer. Dealing with every point does not just mean rolling over – there may be a good reason not to implement a recommended revision. Most reviewers and editors are quite willing to accept, and probably even expect, noncompliance when it is justified by a coherent rationale. Some unsound recommendations may arise from a misreading of the manuscript by a reviewer. In such cases, the error can be pointed out in a nice way, and it is a good policy to change the relevant text to make it less likely that a reader will make the same mistake.

GETTING A HEAD START

When a manuscript or grant proposal is submitted, a candid self-assessment can be valuable in predicting liabilities that may prove problematical in the review process as well as in carrying out future research. I have a vivid memory of my advisor calling a meeting of his research group right after sending off a manuscript for a book. The book provided a theoretical view that encompassed work the individual had carried out for the previous decade. The purpose of the meeting was to identify and discuss *limitations* in the theory described in the manuscript just sent off for publication. My advisor was disparaging, and encouraging others to join in, a book that had not yet made it to the bookshelves. Here the goal was to chart the course of future research, rather than to anticipate a revision because the book already had been accepted for publication. But for manuscripts and grant proposals, the futures of which are in doubt, there may well be an obvious next study to do that can provide a data-based response to a likely future critique. The most powerful weapon to have in debates with reviewers and colleagues is supportive data.

Having had her first taste of disappointment, it is time for my graduate student to roll up her sleeves and get on with the business of rewriting for publication.

REFERENCES

Dennis, W. (1954). Productivity among American psychologists. *American Psychologist, 9*, 191–194.

Dennis, W. (1955). Variations in productivity among creative workers. *Scientific Monthly, 80*, 277–278.

Dennis, W. (1966). Creative productivity between the ages of 20 and 80 years. *Journal of Gerontology, 21*, 1–8.

Simonton, D. K. (1985). Quality, quantity, and age: The careers of 10 distinguished psychologists. *International Journal of Aging and Human Development, 21*, 241–254.

Simonton, D. K. (1988). Quality and purpose, quantity and chance. *Creativity Research Journal, 1*, 68–74.

Simonton, D. K. (1996). Creative expertise: A lifetime developmental perspective. In K. A. Ericsson (Ed.), *The road to excellence: The acquisition of expert performance in the arts and sciences, sports and games* (pp. 227–253). Mahwah, NJ: Erlbaum.

Sternberg, R. J. (1993). *The psychologist's companion: A guide to scientific writing for students and researchers* (3rd ed.). New York: Cambridge University Press.

Sternberg, R. J., Forsythe, G. B., Hedlund, J., Horvath, J., Snook, S. Williams, W. M. Wagner, R. K., & Grigorenko, E. L. (2000). *Practical intelligence in everyday life.* New York: Cambridge University Press.

Sternberg, R. J., & Wagner, R. K. (Eds.) (1986). *Practical intelligence: Nature and origins of competence in the everyday world.* New York: Cambridge University Press.

Wagner, R. K. (1987). Tacit knowledge in everyday intelligent behavior. *Journal of Personality and Social Psychology, 52,* 1236–1247.

Wagner, R. K., & Sternberg, R. J. (1985). Practical intelligence in real-world pursuits: The role of tacit knowledge. *Journal of Personality and Social Psychology, 49,* 436–458.

Wagner, R. K., & Sternberg, R. J. (1987). Tacit knowledge in managerial success. *Journal of Business and Psychology, 1,* 301–312.

PART FOUR

CONCLUSION

Chapter 14

Article Writing 101

A Crib Sheet of 50 Tips for the Final Exam

ROBERT J. STERNBERG

You have now read about how to write articles for publication in psychology and you are ready to prepare for the final exam. The exam is most likely not some multiple-choice delight to be administered at a cramped desk in a college classroom. Rather it is the actual task of writing articles for publication. This final chapter summarizes 50 of the main tips to be distilled from the chapters of this book. Some of the authors suggesting each tip are listed in parentheses in alphabetical order.

GENERAL TIPS

1. *Ask yourself whether your ideas are interesting to you, and why they would be interesting to other people (Tesser):* All of us read articles that leave us gasping for breath: How could anyone find the work interesting other than the author? You are more likely to avoid the embarrassment of proposing boring ideas if you ask yourself why others and not just you should be interested in the ideas you have to offer.

2. *Realize that new ideas are often difficult to get accepted (Sternberg, Tesser):* The more your ideas depart from mainstream ways of thinking, the harder it probably will be to get your ideas accepted. Thus, the more the ideas depart from the mainstream, the more effort you have to devote in your article to convincing people that what you have to say is worth listening to.

3. *Write the article that emerges from your research rather than the article you planned to write (Bem):* It is rare that the research you do leads you to the particular outcomes you expected. Write up the article that best takes into account what you found rather than the one that takes into account what you had hoped to find but never did.

4. *Explore the data to find out what they have to say and not just what you expected them to say (Bem, Grigorenko):* Data often are perverse: They come out a way you did not expect or perhaps never even considered. You should analyze your data to find out what they really tell you rather than only analyzing them for what you thought they might tell you.

5. *A good article tells a story (Eisenberg, Salovey):* You may view story writing as different from professional writing in psychology. In fact, in many ways they are the same. A good psychological article has a story to tell, and develops that story from the beginning to the end, or at least the end as the author knows it.

6. *Write the story the data tell rather than the story of your discovery of the data's story (Bem):* Readers do not want an autobiographical account of how you got to where you are. They just want to know where you are and why.

7. *Write for the student in Psychology 101 (Bem):* Many writers grossly overestimate the background knowledge of their readers. Write an article that any bright introductory-psychology student could understand. Be accurate, clear, well-organized, and direct. Write linearly. Stick to material that elaborates your main story and avoid subplots. Avoid jargon where possible, but if you need it, be sure to define it.

8. *Make clear what is new in your article (Sternberg):* It often is not clear what is new in an article. Make sure you state it directly rather than hoping readers will see it.

9. *Write with your referees in mind (Sternberg):* Think of people likely to review your article and the kinds of objections they are likely to raise. They represent many other readers who may see things differently from you and who need to be convinced of the validity of what you say.

10. *Write in the manner of an hourglass, starting broadly, becoming more specific, and then ending broadly (Bem):* You should start

your article dealing with the broad questions you will address. Then you should get specific in terms of what you did. Finally, you should discuss broadly the implications of your work.

11. *Make clear how your study tests your hypotheses (Kendall et al.):* Sometimes a set of hypotheses is presented and research is presented, but it is not at all obvious how the research actually tests the hypotheses. Make clear how it does.

12. *Polish and proofread (Bem, Eisenberg, Sternberg):* Do not expect referees or editors to do your rewriting for you or to tolerate loose, sloppy, or error-laden writing. Polishing and proofreading are *your* responsibility.

13. *Do not use synonyms, especially for technical terms, just for the sake of avoiding redundancy (Bem):* Readers may believe you are varying the words you use because you are referring to different concepts.

14. *Make length proportional to contribution (Kendall et al.):* Journals have limited space. Longer articles therefore consume a valuable resource. Hence you need to be confident that the longer your article, the greater its contribution.

15. *Use a title that clearly expresses what the article is about and that also, if possible, captures attention (Sternberg):* An irrelevant title tricks people into scanning (but rarely reading) something they do not want to read. A boring title may lead them to avoid reading the article altogether.

16. *Write an abstract that contains the information a reader most would want to know (Sternberg):* Some people never will see anything more than the abstract. The better the abstract captures the key ideas and findings of your article, the better disseminated your work will be.

17. *Accept feedback nondefensively but critically (Wagner, Warren):* Most of the comments you get from referees will help you to produce a better article. Some will not. In revising an article, make the changes that will improve the article. Consider making the changes that, at least, will not hurt the article. But do not make the changes that *will* hurt it. In your letter to the editor, you can explain why you did not make certain changes. The editor, of course, is free to accept or not accept your explanation, as he or she wishes.

18. *A good literature review (whether as a general article or as part of an article) defines and clarifies a problem; summarizes previous research in order to inform the reader of present research; identifies relations, contradictions, gaps, and inconsistencies; and suggests next steps (Eisenberg):* The literature review thus informs readers of where things have been, where they are, and where they need to go.

19. *A good author writes with his or her readers in mind (Eisenberg, Reis):* Write with your readers in mind. Ask yourself how well they will be able to understand what you write. For example, readers often get confused by pronouns without clear antecedents and imprecise language.

20. *A good article has a take-home message (Eisenberg):* Often readers finish an article without any clear idea of what the main point of the article was supposed to be. A good article has a clear take-home message so that the reader briefly can summarize what the article was about.

21. *Write for a class of journals (Eisenberg):* You should have a journal or class of journals in mind when you write an article. The article then can be targeted to the readership and requirements of that journal or class of journals.

22. *Choose carefully the journal to which you submit your article (Warren):* You can save yourself a lot of time by choosing a journal that is appropriate in terms of what it publishes and that is likely to accept an article of the quality yours is.

23. *Do not take reviews personally (Warren):* Reviews are of work, not of you. Some reviewers get personal. Ignore such remarks. Read the reviews in the spirit of using them to improve your article.

24. *When you resubmit an article, be clear as to how you handled each of the points made in the reviews:* Reviewers and editors get annoyed when they are ignored. You should follow most of their suggestions and indicate how you did so in a resubmission letter. Those suggestions you cannot accept should be highlighted in the letter and you should explain why you did not follow them.

25. *Relate what you are writing about to people's everyday experiences (Kendall et al.):* You capture people's attention and inter-

est when you draw the people in by relating what you are studying to experiences they have faced or expect to face in their lives.

26. *Use interesting rhetorical questions (Kendall et al.):* People often find themselves wanting to answer rhetorical questions, thus drawing themselves into the article they are reading.

27. *Say clearly why what you are studying should matter to your readers (Kendall et al.):* Do not expect readers to see on their own the importance of your work. Make clear why the work should matter to them.

28. *Review relevant literature in a way that relates it to the argument you want to make (Kendall et al.):* No one likes to read an unfocused, rambling literature review. Organize your literature review around the ideas that you wish to communicate in your article.

29. *Use direct quotes only when necessary (Kendall et al.):* Use direct quotes only if they are needed to convey the flavor or exact message of an original text. Otherwise, they just clutter up and often obscure your message.

30. *State your research question(s) clearly (Kendall et al., Sternberg):* You need to be very clear just what questions will be addressed in your article. Often you also need to make clear what questions the reader may expect to be addressed that are not, in fact, addressed.

31. *Treat differences of opinion with respect (Kendall et al.):* Treat others the way you would want them to treat you – with respect – even if you disagree with what they say and are convinced that anyone in his or her right mind would see things as you do.

32. *Keep in perspective the importance of your own work (Kendall et al.):* Readers tend to be turned off by authors who glorify the importance of their own work beyond reasonable bounds or who fail to make clear the ways in which their own work builds on the work of others.

33. *Be generous in your citations of others (Smith, Sternberg, Tesser, Wagner):* No one likes to be ignored, especially referees of articles. It therefore is important to cite relevant past work, especially if someone is likely to be a referee of your article. It

further is important to cite work that is not consistent with
your point of view in addition to the work that is consistent.

34. *Be current in your citations of others (Smith):* No one likes
to read an article whose author obviously stopped keeping up
with the field a decade ago. Make sure your citations are current.

35. *Avoid secondary sources (Smith):* Extensive use of secondary
sources suggests laziness on the part of an author. Cite
the primary sources. In this way, you not only show better
scholarship skills, but increase greatly the likelihood that
what you say people said will correspond to what they actually did say.

36. *Actively solicit feedback (Sternberg, Wagner, Warren):* You can
avoid a lot of headaches and heartaches if you anticipate the
comments referees are likely to make before they get a chance
to make them. Ask colleagues to read your work and comment
on it before you submit the work to a journal.

37. *The main elements of design are type of design, how participants were assigned to groups, independent variables, and
dependent variables (Reis):* Make sure your design section contains the necessary elements.

38. *Make clear why the design you chose is appropriate to the problem you have studied (Reis):* Do not expect readers to figure
out why you designed your study as you did.

39. *Make clear what the strengths and limitations of your design are
(Grigorenko, Reis):* Claim only what you can on the basis of
the design you used, and show readers that you know what
appropriate claims are.

40. *Provide top-down structure (Salovey):* It often is difficult for
readers to follow the line of argument in an article. By providing top-down structure and making transparent how you will
organize, you facilitate your readers' understanding of what
you have to say.

41. *Let the story of your data guide your writing of Results, rather
than an arbitrary order based on statistical tests (Salovey):* Do
not write your Results section merely to conform to the order
of output in a bundle of computer outputs. Write in the order
that best conveys the message you wish to convey.

42. *Justify your choices of statistical tests (Grigorenko, Salovey):* Do not assume readers will know why you did the tests you did. Explain why you did them.

43. *Be thorough in your reporting of results without being overwhelming (Grigorenko, Salovey, Sternberg):* Often referees will ask for just those data analyses you chose to omit, so include the full set of data analyses you need to tell your story completely. But omit analyses that are irrelevant to the story you have to tell.

44. *If you cleaned up your data, be clear as to how you did it (Grigorenko):* Say how you handled missing data, outliers, or any other peculiarities in the data, such as non-normality.

45. *Be sure your conclusions follow from your data (Grigorenko, Sternberg):* It is often tempting for an author to go beyond the data in establishing conclusions, saying what he or she wants to conclude rather than what the data allow him or her to conclude. Draw only the proper conclusions, and properly label anything else as speculation.

46. *The Discussion should make clear what you have contributed, how your study helped resolve the original problem, and what conclusions and theoretical implications can be drawn from your study (Calfee):* A good Discussion goes well beyond summarizing the results: It relates your results back to why you originally did the study, and makes clear the meaning of what you found out.

47. *The Discussion should be viewed as argumentation, not just as explanation (Calfee):* Good writing in articles is not merely expository, but persuasive. You are trying to convince readers of the validity of your position, and often, of the lack of validity of alternative positions. However, be realistic in terms of what alternative positions you can rule out.

48. *Decide what is worth emphasizing in your Discussion and what is not (Calfee):* Good writing is hierarchical: It makes clear which the important points are, and which are merely the supporting points.

49. *Use the Discussion to make clear the limitations of your work (Sternberg):* Reviewers will notice them. You take some of the wind out of their sails when you anticipate what they are likely to say in objection to your work.

50. *Never end an article with an expression like "Further research is needed" (Sternberg):* What a bore! Of course further research is needed.

You now are ready to write better articles. The tools are right in this book. You need only use them.

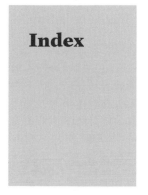

Index